Copyright © 2025 Donna Hamer

All rights reserved. No part of this publication may be reproduced, stored in a retrieval system, or transmitted in any form or by any means — electronic, mechanical, photocopying, recording, or otherwise — without the prior written permission of the copyright owner and publisher.

This book is intended for educational and informational purposes only. The people, events, and insights shared are based on personal experiences, reflections, and research. If you choose to apply any of the concepts within, you do so at your own discretion and assume full responsibility for your actions.

Disclaimer: The content provided in this book is intended for informational and emotional support purposes only. It is not a substitute for professional medical, psychological, veterinary, or legal advice, diagnosis, or treatment. Grieving the loss of a beloved pet is a deeply personal journey, and while the experiences, reflections, and suggestions shared here may offer comfort, each individual's process is unique.

If you are struggling with overwhelming grief, depression, or emotional distress, please seek the guidance of a qualified mental health professional or grief counsellor. Likewise, any references to veterinary care or animal health should not replace consultation with a licensed veterinarian.

The author and publisher disclaim any liability for any loss or risk incurred, directly or indirectly, as a consequence of the use and application of any of the contents of this book.

Your healing matters. Please take what serves you, and leave the rest.

Published by Christine Robinson Global
ISBN: 978-1-7641065-0-4

My Gifts To You

Access Your Support Bonuses using the link below or QR code

https://petlossandgrief.com/book-goodies

https://petlossandgrief.com/book-goodies

Dedication:

I feel truly blessed to be living the life I have. From a young age, I've always been surrounded by animals. I vividly remember the deep love I felt for all of them, from the dogs and cats I brought home to the little kitten with ringworms that I tried to convince my mum needed a home. I recall my dad calling me outside to marvel at a baby water dragon in the yard, the wonder of watching my first foal being born, and even witnessing the birth of a friend's puppies.

Throughout my life, dogs, cats, fish, birds, and horses have always been by my side. I could instinctively sense when my pets were unwell—I felt their pain, their emotions, their stories.

It's no surprise that I've found my purpose in working with animals. It's my dream come true: connecting with them, sharing their messages of love, and honouring the bond we share.

I dedicate this book to all the pets and animals who have shared their lives with me in some way. To the ones who have been with me in my adult life, each of you left an indelible mark, supporting me when I needed it most. To those who have inspired and guided me to write this book, sharing your stories:

> Ajax – my beautiful heart dog, Golden Retriever, passed at 13.5 years
> Fergie – rescued at 9.5 years, Golden Retriever, passed at 16 years
> Chloe – rescued at 9.5 years, Golden Retriever, passed at 13 years
> Lil Jess – rescued at 16 years, Mini Poodle, passed at 19 years
> Spyro – my gorgeous cat
> Ranger – our protector cat
> Speedie – my son's best friend, Mini Foxie
> Kipper – the ultimate lap dog, Tenterfield Terrier
> Teika – my girl, always in my heart
> Ben – my first Golden Retriever, who began it all
> Tabatha – my magic cat

And finally, I dedicate this book to my beautiful son. Never change who you are.

Table Of Contents

Acknowledgement i
Introduction. iii

Chapter 1 1
My Pet Has Passed—Now What? How Do I Go On?

Chapter 2 23
Understanding Pet Loss and Grief

Chapter 3 31
The Stages of Grief in Pet Loss

Chapter 4 37
Coping with Guilt After Pet Loss

Chapter 5 47
Dealing with Blame and Forgiving Yourself

Chapter 6 53
Steps to Process and Heal from Grief

Chapter 7 59
Helping a Pet Cope with the Loss of Another Pet

Chapter 8 63
How Do I Explain My Grief To Friends & Family?

Chapter 9 69
Helping Children Cope with Pet Loss

Chapter 10. 79
　Cremation vs Burying Your Pet

Chapter 11. 85
　Finding Joy and Purpose After Loss

Chapter 12. 89
　How to Honour Your Pet's Memory

Chapter 13. 99
　Will I Ever Feel Normal Again?

Chapter 14. 105
　Signs Your Pet Is Still With You

Chapter 15. 111
　Rituals and Ceremonies for Closure

Chapter 16. 121
　When to Consider A New Pet

Chapter 17. 133
　The Journey Of The Soul Animal

Chapter 18. 143
　Can I Really Communicate With My Pet In Spirit?

Conclusion 153
　Conclusion: A Journey of Love and Healing

Final Message 156
　A Final Message of Comfort and Hope

Acknowledgements

To all the beautiful souls who so generously shared their heartfelt stories of love, loss, and healing — thank you.

Your willingness to open your hearts and speak your truth has breathed life into these pages. Through your vulnerability, you've helped shape a sanctuary for others navigating the pain of losing a beloved animal companion.

Each of your stories carries the spirit of connection, compassion, and deep love that this book was created to honour. Your pets may no longer walk beside you, but their legacy lives on — not only in your hearts, but now in the hearts of every reader this book touches.

This book is as much yours as it is mine. Thank you for helping others heal by bravely sharing your journey.

With deepest gratitude,

Donna Hamer

Tanya and Latte
Candy and Silvia
Eve and Anne
Cheri and Rocki
Wendy and Hermie
Nadine and Chance
Joanne and Joey
Lisa and Team Golden Oldies
Jaya and Kayla
Sharon and Rosie & Hank
Sarah and Harvey & Kali
Alan and Mia
Anita and Wentworth & Griffin

Introduction

Losing a pet is one of the most profound heartbreaks we may ever face. For those who've shared their lives with an animal companion, it's not just losing a pet—it's losing a best friend, a buddy, someone you can share with, and a source of unconditional love. This loss can leave a void that feels impossible to fill.

As an animal communicator, I've devoted my life to understanding the deep and enduring connections between humans and their pets. From an early age, I discovered my intuitive ability to connect with animals, both living and in spirit. Over the years, I've had the privilege of working with countless pet parents, helping them find solace and reassurance after the loss of a beloved companion.

I've also experienced this grief first hand, having said goodbye to six of my own cherished pets in the last six years. Each loss was different, and while you might think that my daily work in pet loss and grief would make it easier, it doesn't. These experiences, both personal and professional, have only reinforced what I know to be true: the bond we share with our pets is unbreakable, even after they've crossed the Rainbow Bridge.

This book is for you—the pet parent who feels lost, overwhelmed, or unsure how to move forward. Whether your loss is recent or years old, whether it was sudden or anticipated, your grief is valid. I hope that this book will provide comfort, understanding, and practical tools to help you navigate this journey.

"Journey" What Does This Mean?

Life's journey is filled with wonder, challenges, heartbreaks, soaring highs, and painful lows. It's defined by celebrations, special moments, and memories that shape our experience as humans. These events, whether planned or unexpected, impact us deeply, guiding us and shaping our purpose.

'Pet loss and Grief' is also a journey, one without a clear beginning or end. One day, you might feel like you're handling it well, and the next, it hits you all over again. This ebb and flow is a natural part of grief, and there's no timeline for healing.

This book is designed to be a companion for anyone navigating the difficult path of pet loss. It offers a compassionate space to process your emotions, understand your feelings, and find ways to heal while honouring the love and life you shared with your pet.

You Might Be Asking Yourself

- 'Did I do the right thing?'
- 'Why does this hurt so much?'
- 'How can I go on without them?'
- 'Will I ever feel normal again?'

These are just some of the questions I hear every day in my animal communication sessions—questions rooted in love, guilt, and a deep longing to understand and honour the bond you shared with your pet.

Together, we'll explore the many dimensions of pet loss, from the raw pain of goodbye to the bittersweet joy of remembering. I'll also share ways to connect with your pet in spirit, offering reassurance that the love you shared continues to exist in powerful and meaningful ways.

Introduction

Grief is a journey, not a destination. It's a process of learning to carry the love and memories of your pet with you as you move forward. You don't have to navigate this journey alone. Let this book be your companion, offering support and solace as you honour the life and love of your cherished animal friend.

How This Book Can Support You

Grieving the loss of a pet can feel isolating, especially when others may not fully understand the depth of your pain. This book is here to remind you that you're not alone and offers:

- Practical guidance for navigating the grieving process.
- Tools for coping with guilt, blame, and the 'what ifs'.
- Stories and insights to help you feel less alone.
- Ways to honour your pet's memory and keep their spirit alive.
- Stories of healing from others who've walked this path.
- Reassurance that the bond you shared with your pet continues, even after their passing.

Using This Book

This book includes exercises to support you on your journey. You'll find journal prompts to help you reflect and process your emotions. Whether you choose to buy a special journal and some colourful pens to write with or simply grab a piece of paper and jot down notes, there's no right or wrong way to approach this. This is *your* journey, and the exercises and prompts are designed to guide you in the way that feels most meaningful and comfortable for you.

Take your time. Flip through the book, read a chapter, sit with what comes up for you, and try the exercises or journaling. There's no rush—this isn't a process you need to complete in a day, a week, or even a month. Each chapter represents a small step on the path of your pet loss and grief journey.

My Hope For You

By the end of this journey, I hope that you'll feel comforted, supported, and empowered to move forward, carrying your pet's love with you every step of the way.

Chapter 1

My Pet Has Passed—Now What? How Do I Go On?

Losing a beloved pet shakes your entire world. One moment they're there — offering unconditional love, comfort, and companionship — and the next, the silence feels deafening. Whether the loss happened suddenly or after a long goodbye, the absence they leave behind can feel overwhelming and all-consuming.

In these early days, grief may come in waves. You might feel disoriented, heavy with sadness, or even numb. These emotions are natural. They reflect how deeply you loved and how much your companion meant to you.

This chapter will walk you through the first tender steps after saying goodbye. You'll find comfort, clarity, and gentle guidance, so you never feel alone in this journey. Grief may change your world, but you don't have to walk through it without support.

Facing the Immediate Aftermath of Loss

In the moments and days following your pet's passing, emotions may overwhelm you. Shock, disbelief, sadness, and even numbness are all natural reactions. You might ask, 'Did I do the right thing?' This question is common if you have to make the heartbreaking decision to euthanise your pet.

Know that your decision came from love—a deep, selfless love prioritising your pet's comfort and peace. Euthanasia is one of the hardest choices a pet parent can make. Picking up the phone to arrange a vet visit or saying yes to the vet in their office is one of the most challenging decisions you'll make. Still, it's also the greatest act of kindness we can offer when a pet's suffering becomes too much.

Sudden Loss vs Expected Passing

The way we process grief can vary depending on the circumstances of our pet's passing:

- **Sudden Loss:** When a pet's passing is unexpected, the shock can feel unbearable. One moment, everything feels normal, and the next, your world is forever changed. You may replay the events leading up to their loss, searching for answers or signs you might have missed.

It's essential to allow yourself to feel these emotions without judgement. Grief is not linear, and the sudden nature of the loss may mean it takes longer to process.

- **An Illness or Expected Passing:** When a pet has been unwell, their passing, though anticipated, can still feel deeply painful.

Knowing their time was approaching may have allowed you to prepare on some level, but it doesn't ease the ache of saying goodbye.

Forms of Grief in Pet Loss

Grief can hit us anytime, any place, it doesn't discriminate. It may begin before your pet passes, immediately after their passing, or even years later. It may arise when your pet goes missing, or you have to surrender them as you can no longer care for them, or when a sudden or traumatic loss occurs. There are many different forms of grief, each uniquely impacting and shaping our grieving process.

Normal Grief - Normal grief is the typical, healthy response to loss, involving a range of emotions such as sadness, anger, guilt, and eventually, acceptance. While grief never entirely disappears, over time, it becomes more manageable as we adjust to life without our pet.

Anticipatory Grief - This is the deep sadness we feel when we know the loss of a beloved pet is inevitable. It often begins with a terminal diagnosis, the natural decline of age, or a planned goodbye, such as euthanasia. The emotions can be just as intense as grief after loss, as we begin to process the reality of parting before it happens.

Disenfranchised Grief - When a loss is not recognised or validated by others, grief can feel isolating. This happens when a pet goes missing, is rehomed, or is lost under circumstances others may not understand. It can leave pet parents feeling as though they have no right to grieve, when in reality, their pain is just as real and deserving of acknowledgment.

Traumatic Grief - Grief often hits hardest when a pet's passing happens suddenly, through an accident, injury, or other traumatic event. The shock can trigger intense emotional responses, including symptoms of post-traumatic stress (PTSD). Because the mind and body struggle to make sense of such an abrupt loss, healing may take longer and require deeper support.

Complicated Grief - Also known as prolonged or persistent grief, this involves intense emotions that do not lessen over time and may interfere with daily life. If, after a year or more, grief continues to feel overwhelming and unbearable, it may be helpful to seek support from a counsellor or pet loss specialist.

Normal Grief

Grieving the loss of a pet is a normal and natural process, much like mourning the death of a human loved one. The emotions that arise—sadness, loneliness, anger, guilt—can sometimes feel overwhelming. Many people don't fully realise how much their pets shape their daily lives until they are gone. Our pets give us purpose, companionship, and unconditional love. They are part of our routines, our quiet moments, and our joy. When they pass, they leave behind memories and an emptiness that only they once filled.

It's natural to experience a range of emotions—shock, denial, anger, guilt, or even bargaining. Grief can also manifest physically, leading to exhaustion, changes in appetite, and difficulty sleeping. Everyone processes loss in their own way, and there is no right or wrong way to grieve.

Allow yourself time to feel whatever emotions come up. It's okay to be sad, to cry, to feel angry, or lost. Your grief is valid, and your love for your pet doesn't disappear just because they are no longer physically with you.

While this is the experience of normal grief, other forms of grief can arise when facing the end of life with a pet, some of which may take you by surprise. In the next section, we'll explore the different ways grief can manifest and how each experience is unique.

Anticipatory Grief and Disenfranchised Grief are often misunderstood, yet can have a profound impact.

Anticipatory Grief

Many guardians don't realise they are experiencing grief before their pet has even passed. This grief can manifest as fatigue, overwhelm, and constant worry as they navigate the emotional weight of knowing their beloved companion's time is limited.

 **Tia**

A client shared with me, "I always thought Latte would pass first. When Tia passed before her, it left me questioning why every single day. Now I'm planning to go on holiday, but I'm terrified. What if Latte passes while I'm away? I'm worried all the time."

We took some time to explore her feelings, and she began to recognise that what she was experiencing was anticipatory grief—the emotional weight of not knowing when her dog might pass. It's easy for someone to say, "Don't worry," but worrying comes naturally to those who see their pets as babies.

We talked about how this constant fear was impacting her. I suggested a shift in focus: instead of fearing the inevitable, try to live in the now, cherishing the precious moments. "Enjoy the time you have together," I encouraged her. "Don't let the fear of what's to come overshadow the joy of the present."

This simple reframing can help create a space where love and connection take centre stage, even in the face of uncertainty.

Anticipatory grief can be emotionally complex because you're mourning your pet while they're still with you. It may bring waves of sadness, guilt, fear, and helplessness, alongside moments of joy as you cherish the time you have left together.

How It Affects You:

- **Emotional Strain:** Guilt over decisions or worry about your pet's comfort.
- **Physical Impact**: Fatigue, sleeplessness, and physical aches.
- **Mental Overload:** Anxiety, overthinking, and constant worry.
- **Conflicting Emotions:** Joy in their presence one moment, profound sadness the next.

Recognising anticipatory grief allows you to offer yourself compassion during this difficult time. Seeking support can lighten the emotional load and help you honour your pet's final days with love, presence, and care.

Even after your pet has passed, you may continue to experience elements of anticipatory grief, especially if they had a prolonged illness and you had been preparing for their passing. You might still find yourself grappling with the reality of life without them and the complex emotions tied to that transition, even after the loss has occurred. This can manifest in several ways, including revisiting the "what ifs," processing the circumstances of their passing, and coming to terms with the depth of the loss.

Eve

Looking back, my biggest takeaway as an anticipatory griever who has since lost her pet: all the grief and what-ifs didn't ease the loss. I wasted precious time grieving her while she was still here, and it did not make losing her any easier. It didn't prepare me for the devastation of the loss that has sent shock waves through my entire life in the months since she passed.

As someone who suffers from anxiety, whose mind is always filled with intrusive thoughts, now when I start anticipating the losses of my remaining pets, I redirect my thinking into how special the current moment is—how sweet and cute and funny they're being right now and how happy that makes me feel inside. I turn tears into kisses. I'm sure this annoys my doggies, but I give them anyway as it makes me smile.

My heart hurts all the time after losing my precious baby, my soul dog, but it's the price we pay for their love and companionship. Please don't make yourself start paying that price early, because you deserve to feel happy and enjoy your time with them. Give your pup a big kiss from me ♥. Senior dogs are such gifts. I also found therapy to be an absolute game changer to help me deal with the grief, talking to someone who understands how you feel and doesn't judge you made such a difference.

Candy

I've had to say goodbye to many pets in my lifetime—some suddenly, without warning, others over long, agonising periods filled with anticipatory grief. Twice, I've experienced the slow, heart-wrenching process of knowing the end was coming but not knowing exactly when or how. It feels like your heart is being ripped from your chest, piece by piece. You wait, hope, pray, and bargain with the universe, clinging to any chance that time might stretch just a little longer. It's grieving before the grieving truly begins.

For me, the mourning started the moment I received the news that my cats were terminally ill. The initial shock was paralysing, but my instinct was to become overly practical—researching cremation options, choosing urns, and planning for euthanasia. I buried myself in logistics, convincing myself that if I took care of the details first, I could somehow keep my emotions at bay. But once everything was arranged, there was nowhere left to hide. The grief I had been holding at arm's length came flooding in.

Those final days were a whirlwind of mixed emotions. I desperately wanted more time, yet I couldn't bear to see them suffer. I tried to stay present, not letting my mind race to the loneliness that awaited me. Instead, I focused on the moments still left to savour—the warmth of the sun as we curled up on the grass together, the gentle weight of their paws in my hand as they slept. I captured these moments in photos, made paw prints as keepsakes, prepared their favourite meals, and gave friends and family the chance to say goodbye.

> There were plenty of tears, sleepless nights, and overwhelming sadness. But having a plan in place gave me the space to be with them in those final days. It allowed me to set aside my heartbreak and focus on ensuring they felt nothing but love and comfort. And when I said goodbye, I knew I had given them everything I could.
>
> The grief didn't end there, of course. It never does. But I take solace in knowing that deep, unconditional love never truly fades. It lingers in the memories, the quiet moments, and the undeniable presence of our bond.

Disenfranchised Grief – When Grief Feels Invisible

There are many situations where pet parents experience disenfranchised grief:

A pet going missing – When a beloved pet disappears, whether they wander away, are stolen, or vanish, the heartbreak is immense. Without closure, the grief can feel endless, and yet, others may not understand the weight of this loss.

Having to rehome a pet – Life circumstances sometimes force people to make the painful decision to rehome their pet. The guilt, sadness, and longing can be overwhelming, yet this grief is rarely acknowledged by those who have never been in that position.

The loss of a pet that others did not know – If your pet was your private companion, rarely seen by others, you might feel like no one truly understands your loss. But you do. Your love was real, and so is your grief.

Grieving a pet that was not a traditional companion – People deeply bond with all kinds of animals—birds, reptiles, rabbits, farm animals, and even insects. Yet society often minimises these losses, failing to see the depth of love that existed.

The passing of a foster pet – Loving and caring for a foster animal, even temporarily, creates a connection. Saying Goodbye can be just as painful, but it is rarely acknowledged in the same way as losing a longtime pet.

Th loss of a working or service animal – Whether a guide dog, therapy animal, or farm companion, these animals play vital roles in our lives. Losing them is not just losing a pet—it is losing a partner, a source of support, and a deep emotional bond.

Grieving in a world that doesn't understand – Hearing phrases like "It was just a dog" or "You can get another one" can be harrowing. These words diminish our love and connection with our animals, making us feel even more isolated in our grief.

Facing financial limitations – There's no denying the depth of love we hold for our pets, and we often go to great lengths to provide them with the very best. When illness strikes and the cost of treatment becomes more than we can handle, some may feel they have no choice but to choose euthanasia. This heartbreaking decision can leave behind a deep well of grief, often complicated by guilt, helplessness, and the painful belief that others won't truly understand.

Making the decision to euthanise – Ending a beloved pet's life is one of the most heartbreaking decisions a person can face. The weight of this choice often lingers long after the moment has passed, bringing with it waves of doubt and guilt. Many are left wondering, *'Did I do the right thing? Was it too soon?'* This inner turmoil can lead to disenfranchised grief, especially when others don't fully understand the depth of the bond or the pain of making such a decision. Some may even question whether the choice was made out of compassion for their pet, or because their own emotional or physical strength had reached its limit. It's a layered, complex grief, and often carried in silence.

If you are experiencing disenfranchised grief, please know that your pain is real, and your love for your pet was, and still is, deeply meaningful. There is no "right" or "wrong" way to grieve, and no one else has the power to tell you whether your grief is valid.

 The Grief of the Unseen Goodbye

The feral cat I had been caring for disappeared. At first, I told myself it was temporary—feral cats wander. But as the days stretched on, anxiety crept in.

What if she's been hit by a car? What if she's trapped somewhere? What if she's never coming back?

Just as my heart started to break, she returned—thinner but unharmed. Relief flooded me, and we fell back into our rhythm. I had built her shelters, offered her food, and though she came and went as she pleased, she had chosen me.

Rocki wasn't just another stray. She was special.

She arrived one summer day, bringing tiny kittens into my yard. It was a joy I hadn't felt since childhood, a second chance after my parents took my first kittens away when I was young. But my husband didn't share my excitement. He insisted they couldn't stay. His dismissive comments stung, but I had no choice—I found them homes, even though my gut told me they weren't ready to leave their mother.

Rocki grieved. She searched for them, crying for days. And I grieved with her, the pain was unbearable.

Eventually, she adjusted, slipping back into her independent life. I wished things had been different, but I clung to the

> comfort that at least she was still here. Then, one day before Thanksgiving, she finished her meal, cleaned herself in the neighbour's yard, and looked back at me. I didn't know it would be the last time I'd ever see her.
>
> I have grieved ever since. Without closure, without answers, and without the world fully understanding. To some, she was "just a feral cat." But grief doesn't care about labels.
>
> She shared a part of her life with me. And I loved her.

Traumatic Grief or Complicated Grief

Due to the complexities of Traumatic Grief or Complicated Grief, please seek support from a counsellor or pet loss specialist. You do not have to carry this pain alone. There is strength in reaching out; healing does not mean forgetting—it means learning to carry the love alongside the loss.

> **Traumatic Grief After Pet Loss**
>
> I received a message from a woman whose beloved dog had passed away after a tragic accident over a year ago, her pain was still raw. She described constant exhaustion, frequent tears, and a deep struggle to function in daily life. Although she had seen a grief counsellor, her heart still felt heavy.
>
> What she was experiencing was traumatic grief—a kind of grief that overwhelms the mind, body, and spirit, especially when the loss is sudden, distressing, or deeply personal.

> She was full of guilt and self-blame, questioning whether her dog's passing was her fault and wondering if he had reincarnated. These thoughts had become heavy burdens she couldn't put down. She asked if an animal communication session could help, and whether I would be honest with her—especially about those two things.
>
> I told her this: sometimes, our grief can act like a fog. It doesn't mean our pets in spirit aren't with us—it just means our pain makes it harder to feel them. I gently explained that reincarnation is a soul choice, and not every pet returns in this lifetime. If they don't come back, it isn't punishment. It's simply part of their soul's journey.
>
> I encouraged her to keep speaking with her counsellor, and to consider journalling—writing about happy memories, the bond they shared, and moments that made her smile. This simple practice can begin to shift the focus from loss to love.
>
> And finally, I told her that when she could speak her dog's name without tears every time, that might be the right moment to book in an animal communication session—when her heart was just a little more ready to receive the love he still offers her from the other side.
>
> Grief isn't something we move on from—it's something we learn to carry differently. And when we stop carrying it alone, healing can begin.

No matter what form your grief takes, it is valid. Your love for your pet was deep, and so is the sorrow that follows their absence. Be gentle with yourself as you navigate this journey. Grief is not something to be rushed, ignored, or compared—it is a profoundly personal experience that unfolds in its own time.

Each pet leaves a unique paw print on our hearts, a bond transcending time and space. Though their physical presence may be gone, the love you shared will always remain, woven into the fabric of your soul.

You are not alone. Your grief matters. And most of all, **your love continues.**

Carer's Fatigue

Caring for a sick pet can be emotionally, physically, and mentally exhausting, yet we often don't realise we're experiencing carer's fatigue. The daily cycle of watching, waiting, worrying, checking their breathing, and monitoring every small change can take a toll that lingers even after our pet has passed.

Carer's fatigue, also known as caregiver burnout, arises when the demands of caregiving become overwhelming, leaving little room for self-care. It's a state of profound, bone-level exhaustion that drains not just your body, but your heart, spirit, and sense of self.

While carer's fatigue can mirror many of the same symptoms as anticipatory grief, such as sadness, anxiety, and emotional depletion, they are not quite the same. Anticipatory grief is the sorrow we begin to feel when we know a loss is coming, while carer's fatigue stems from the ongoing strain of daily responsibilities and emotional toil we experience. Both can exist simultaneously, and often do, making it important to acknowledge and care for both the emotional and physical aspects of your experience.

Understanding this fatigue is essential, as its effects can persist long after your pet is gone. Recognising the signs and finding ways to support yourself can help you process your grief while also honouring the love and devotion you gave so selflessly.

When looking after a sick pet, carer fatigue can manifest in several ways:

1. **Emotional Strain:** Caring for a pet who is unwell often comes with intense emotions—fear for their wellbeing, sadness over their condition, guilt over decisions about their care, and even frustration with the challenges of their illness.

2. **Physical Exhaustion:** Long nights, disrupted sleep, or constant vigilance can leave you physically drained. Administering medications, managing symptoms, or providing round-the-clock care can take a toll on your energy.

3. **Mental Overload:** The worry of "Am I doing enough?" or "Am I making the right decisions?" can lead to overthinking and mental exhaustion.

4. **Neglecting Self-Care:** It's common for caregivers to put their pet's needs above their own, skipping meals, sleep, or time to relax. Over time, this imbalance can lead to burnout.

5. **Feelings of Isolation:** Some people feel alone in their caregiving journey, especially if others around them don't fully understand the bond they share with their pet or the intensity of their responsibilities.

How to Manage Carer's Fatigue While Caring for a Sick Pet:

- **Set Boundaries:** Recognise that you can't do everything. Permit yourself to take breaks, even if it's just for a few moments of quiet time.

- **Ask for Help:** Reach out to friends, family, or your veterinarian for support—you don't have to carry this burden alone. I understand that asking for help can be difficult, but remember, if you become overwhelmed or burned out, who will be there for your pet? Taking care of yourself is just as important as caring for them.

- **Prioritise Self-Care:** Caring for yourself isn't selfish—it's necessary. Make time to rest, eat, and recharge so that you can continue to care for your pet effectively.

- **Talk to Others:** Connecting with others who understand the emotional toll of caring for a sick pet can provide comfort and reassurance.

Caring for a sick pet is a profound act of love, but it's essential to remember that your well-being matters too. Taking steps to manage carer's fatigue can help you show up for your pet with the love and care they need while also taking care of yourself.

 **Anne**

One client shared that the stress of caring for her elderly dog led to dangerously high blood pressure, as she always felt stressed. When her pet passed, she felt an initial sense of relief, followed by guilt for feeling that way. After our conversation, she took steps to prioritise her self-care. Acknowledging that she did her best and that no amount of stress and worry would change the outcome.

The 'Relief–Guilt' is a cycle that can be overwhelming. It's essential to recognise that relief is a natural response to the end of prolonged stress and worry.

When guilt arises, remind yourself that you did your best. Your love, care, and presence brought them comfort and dignity in their final days, a testament to the bond you shared.

Lil Jess

In a whirlwind moment, I volunteered to care for a senior Poodle named Lil Jess while her elderly mum was hospitalised for a hip operation. What was supposed to be just one week turned into six months. When the mum didn't return home, her family decided to give Lil Jess away. I couldn't bear the thought of her being passed to strangers, as she was 'a little old lady' who deserved love and care in her senior years, so I stepped in to give her that.

Lil Jess came with a long list of health challenges: skin issues, Cushing's disease, a severe 6/6 heart murmur, and the effects of old age, which had left her blind and deaf. For three years, I navigated the emotional rollercoaster of **anticipatory grief** and **carer's fatigue**, never knowing if she'd still be with me when I woke each morning.

Sometimes she would wander to the bathroom where I kept a doggie toilet mat at night. Other times, she would wake me barking —or I'd wake instinctively, knowing she needed to toilet. Right up until the end, she was fiercely independent. Often, I'd wake to find her distressed, lost in another room, unable to find her way back to her little bed. Many nights she woke me at 4 am, needing to do more than just a wee, so outside we would head. Afterwards, she'd walk to the fridge and indicate she needed food before happily going back to sleep, leaving me wide awake, unable to drift off again.

Our vet joked that she might live forever because her Cushing's disease made her constantly hungry. One morning, I came downstairs and saw her lying completely still on the kitchen floor. My heart sank—I thought she had passed. But as soon as I opened the fridge door, she jumped up and trotted over. Despite being completely deaf, she somehow always knew when food was involved!

In her final days, Lil Jess began chewing on her front legs, creating wounds that quickly became infected. Despite antibiotics and bandages to keep them covered, she always found a way to remove the wrappings, and the wounds worsened. Realising her body was going into sepsis and that she would soon be in unbearable pain, I consulted with the vet and made the heartbreaking decision to help her transition peacefully.

I had hoped she might pass naturally in her sleep at the remarkable age of 19, but I knew deep down that waiting any longer would have caused her unnecessary suffering. Letting her go was one of the hardest decisions I've ever made, but I took comfort in knowing that I had given her the love, dignity, and care she deserved right up until her final moments.

On the drive to the vets, the car started playing up and at one point cut out. I felt the weight of the world on my shoulders as I was deciding for another being's life.

Afterwards, I came home and cried. I cried for the life she had missed out on. I cried for the space she left behind. And I cried from the relief of no longer questioning myself every day, wondering if I was doing the right thing for her. For weeks after her passing, I still woke up in the middle of the night, instinctively checking on her.

> Caring for Lil Jess taught me the depths of love, the weight of responsibility, and the emotional toll of balancing anticipatory grief with carer's fatigue. Despite the challenges, I wouldn't trade those years with her for anything. They were filled with moments of humour (she made me laugh with her funny little antics), the resilience elderly pets have, and the unconditional love she showed me.

Creating Space for Grief

Grieving the loss of your pet isn't something you need to "get over" or rush through. Grief is a reflection of love, and healing has no timeline. Allow yourself the freedom to:

- Cry as much as you need to. Someone once said to me, "I can't cry, is there something wrong with me"? Not crying doesn't mean there's something wrong with you. Grief shows up in many ways, and everyone processes it differently. Some people cry easily, while others don't—and that's okay. It doesn't mean you loved your pet any less or that your grief isn't real.

  Crying is just one way to express emotion, and grief can also appear as exhaustion, numbness, anxiety, anger, or even a sense of disbelief. Sometimes, your body protects you by holding back tears until you feel ready. Try watching a sad movie; this always brings up emotions and allows the tears to flow for me.

- Keep their favourite toy, blanket, or bed nearby for comfort. Holding them or cuddling these items can bring relief in the moment.

- Share your feelings with someone who understands and won't judge you, whether it's friends, family, or a support group.

I kept my golden retriever's bed for a year after his passing—it sat in the corner; I just wasn't ready to part with it. Every morning, I would come downstairs and look at his bed and smile, remembering how much he loved that bed.

A client told me she bought two teddies just before her dog passed. When the time came, she placed one teddy with her beloved dog, so she'd have something to cuddle on her journey. The other she kept for herself, a tender reminder to hold close whenever she needed comfort or wanted to feel near her dog again.

Many pet parents I've worked with carry small urns or keepsakes to keep their pets close. Whatever helps you feel connected is valid.

There's no "right" way to grieve—it's your journey, and however you experience it is valid.

Practical Steps to Begin Healing

While grief may feel all-consuming, small steps can help you navigate the pain:

Honour Their Memory: Create a meaningful ritual or space to celebrate your pet's life. Light a candle, frame a favourite photo, or keep a piece of their hair with you. After Ajax passed, a friend gifted me a beautiful white orchid. It bloomed for months, and when it reflowered about six months later, it felt like a gentle reminder that he was still close to me.

Honouring their memory doesn't have to happen right away. You might feel inspired on an anniversary, a special day, or simply when the moment feels right. Honour their memory in a way that brings you comfort and peace.

Lean on Support Systems: Reach out to others who understand your loss. Online and local communities for pet loss can be a lifeline. However, staying in these groups long term can sometimes prolong emotional pain. Listen to your heart, stepping away is okay when it feels like the group is no longer helping.

Take Care of Yourself: Grief takes a toll on your mind and body. Prioritise rest, proper nutrition, and self-care. Take some time off work to allow yourself the space to process your emotions. Consider a healing or massage to help release "held-in emotions".

It's not uncommon to suffer from sleep disorders, loss of appetite, or various pains. Please seek professional help if you experience these symptoms.

Seeking Support: Knowing When to Reach Out

If the weight of your grief feels too heavy to bear alone, reaching out for professional support can provide a safe space to process your emotions. Pet loss counsellors and therapists specialise in this unique form of grief and can help guide you through the healing process.

Remember, the love you shared with your pet doesn't end with their passing—it lives on in your memories, your heart, and the life you shared. Take this journey one step at a time, allowing yourself to feel, heal, and honour the beautiful bond that will forever be a part of you.

PET LOSS AND GRIEF

Connie Lane recommends **Donna DoLittle - Animal Communicator**.
April 14 at 6:35 AM

It's been 4 weeks since my boy left me. 🐾. Never did it ever cross my mind that walking into the vet and 2 hours later walking out with him. My whole world has been ripped apart. I couldn't comprehend what had happened, I couldn't process it. Those 2 hours just kept haunting me. Over and over. I was desperate for answers as I didn't get any from the vet. My boy was only 7. . Then I came across Donna, and immediately booked a zoom call. And it's been a week since that call. I'm not sure even how to express what this call did to me.... For me..
My boy was waiting for me. Donna connected with Teddy and there was tears, laughter and more tears. Donna relayed things within the first few mins that no one knew. I went into the call desperately wanting to connect to my boy and get answers and I did. I honestly can't thank you enough Donna. You have an amazing gift and bringing my Teddy to me is something I will never ever forget. 🐾. And I will definitely check in with him again..

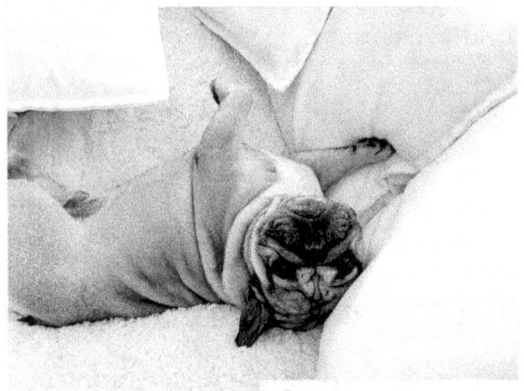

Brian Sturgeon recommends **Donna DoLittle - Animal Communicator**.
December 6, 2022

Highly Recommend Donna DoLittle.
Met Donna at the Noosaville Pet Expo 2022.

Contacted Donna in an Emergency situation, involving an 8 Week old Miniture galloway that had been bitten by a Paralysis tick. The Calf's Mother had mourned the passing of her calf.

3 Days later, the Calf moved its ear and tail.

With the assistance of Donna and her amazing healing and communication abilities, The Calf after 10 days, is now back functioning to her normal self.
Her Mother has accepted her back and is nursing her to a full recovery.

Highly recommend Donna.
Even if You are Sceptic, this experience will bring tears to your eyes.

Thanks again Donna.

Brian Sturgeon.
Kalimna White Swiss Shepherds.

Donna Hamer and 4 others — 5 comments

Chapter 2

Understanding Pet Loss and Grief

Why Pet Loss Feels So Overwhelming

The loss of a pet can be as devastating as losing a human family member, yet society often fails to recognise it as a significant loss. Pets are not just animals; they are our companions, confidants, and the source of unwavering, unconditional love. They listen without judgment, comfort us in our darkest moments, and bring joy to our everyday lives. It can feel like a piece of your heart is missing when they pass. This grief is deeply personal, and because others often misunderstand it, it can feel even more isolating.

For many, the pain of pet loss is compounded by the circumstances surrounding it. A sudden loss can leave you in shock, grappling with unanswered questions and a flood of what-ifs. Taking your pet to the vet for what you thought was a routine visit, only to return home without them, can leave you blindsided and unprepared. These moments create an overwhelming sense of emptiness and loss that can feel impossible to process.

I'll never forget the day I took my beautiful Golden Retriever, Chloe, to the weekend vet. She was 13, and her back legs had given out again—something that had happened a year before, so I felt this was a fairly routine matter. I wasn't too worried as she was her usual happy self, and I planned to see my regular vet the next working day for more pain relief and acupuncture. But when we carried her into the surgery, the vet looked at me and said, "It's time to let her go."

I stared at him in disbelief. "What?" I asked, hoping I'd misunderstood. But he repeated it: "It's time to let her go." I felt enormous pressure, I didn't get a chance to decide, and I wasn't asked. I was told, 'It's time!'

Nothing could have prepared me for those words. I wasn't ready—not even close. The tears flowed uncontrollably as I sat with her for some time, trying to process what was happening. I stayed by her side until the very end, but walking out of that clinic an hour later without her was one of the hardest moments of my life.

For days afterwards, I was lost in a fog of grief. I couldn't stop replaying the moment, trying to understand what I had missed. My other dogs sat quietly with me, offering their silent, comforting presence while I cried and wanted to understand everything. The overwhelming feeling I felt in that moment, hearing those words, was like nothing I'd ever experienced before. It took time even to begin to process the depth of that loss.

How Society Perceives Pet Loss

One of the most challenging aspects of grieving a pet is how society often minimises the loss. When a person passes away, rituals and customs are in place to acknowledge the grief, funerals, condolences, and a general understanding that the bereaved will need time to heal. In contrast, society's response can be dismissive when a pet dies. Comments like "It was just a dog" or "You can always get another one" can invalidate your pain and make you feel isolated.

This lack of acknowledgment can lead many pet parents to hide their grief, fearing judgment or misunderstanding. They may bottle up their feelings, putting on a brave face in public while privately struggling with the depth of their sorrow. This unexpressed grief can become even heavier to bear, especially when it resurfaces unexpectedly during subsequent losses or triggers memories of previous pets who have passed.

The Unique Challenges of Losing a Pet

Losing a pet comes with its challenges that make the grief deeply personal and often misunderstood. Pets are woven into the fabric of our daily lives, from morning walks to bedtime snuggles, and their absence is felt in every quiet space they once filled. Losing these routines can leave you feeling unmoored and unsure how to navigate life without them.

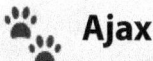

Ajax

When my beautiful Golden Retriever, Ajax, passed away early one morning, I was consumed by so much guilt that I didn't know how to deal with his passing. He had cancer, and I had nursed him for 48 hours as he slowly slipped away from me.

After he passed, I stopped walking altogether. I couldn't bear the thought of walking through our neighbourhood where people might ask about him. I wasn't ready to explain, and truthfully, I wasn't prepared to face the reality of his absence. Everything I once did with him felt unbearable, going for our morning walk, our usual morning routine at the coffee shop, laughing and talking to family, friends, and neighbours about him.

> Ajax was my soul mate; he was my everything, and his passing hit me so hard that I struggled to see how to continue living without him.
>
> In the days following Ajax's passing, I felt utterly lost. I'd sit for hours surfing the internet, not knowing what I was looking for, simply trying to escape the ache in my heart. Hours would pass, and I'd still be sitting in the same spot, unable to move. I felt empty, like a piece of me had been taken away forever.

A sudden loss can be especially traumatic. Taking a pet to the vet for what seems like a routine visit, only to leave without them, can feel like a sucker punch to the soul. The shock of the moment—the unexpected goodbye—leaves you raw, unprepared, and emotionally shattered.

The grief of losing a pet isn't just about their absence; it's about losing the companionship, the routines, and the unconditional love that they gave so freely. It's okay to feel lost, and it's okay to take time to heal. Remember, you're not alone on this journey.

Acknowledging Your Feelings as Valid and Real

It is crucial to acknowledge that your grief is valid. Losing a pet is a significant loss, and it's okay to feel deeply affected by it. Your feelings are a testament to the love and bond you shared with your pet. Allow yourself to grieve in whatever way feels natural to you, whether that's crying, talking loudly to your pet (even if you think they can't hear you), sharing about them with whoever will listen, or finding ways to honour their memory.

Letting Hermie Go

Hermie came into my life in 2010 as a tiny tan dachshund puppy. I'd had a dachshund as a child, but while he was "mine," he quickly became my mother's dog. Hermie, however, was truly mine—and I've always felt he came into my life for a reason.

He was somewhere between a mini and a standard dachshund, but to me, he was perfect. Opinionated and single-minded like most dachshunds, Hermie had a big personality. He shared my emotional pain during some tough years, even mirroring my health issues, including gallbladder problems. He also had arthritis and, later, medication-induced Cushing's disease from years of anti-itch meds. Being allergic to grass and dust was not ideal for a farm dog. Hermie loved being active, though he was food-obsessed and prone to weight gain. By the end, he was on a cocktail of medications to keep him comfortable.

When he turned 13, his health declined sharply. He needed major dental work, which, in hindsight, may have been too much. While he briefly rallied, his decline was quick. At 13½, we knew it was time. I had known it was getting closer all the time, but like so many pet parents, any small burst of energy or enthusiasm for life was seized upon as a reason to wait a little longer. Did we wait too long? Very possibly.

That day, I had to visit my elderly father and didn't mention Hermie as I knew I couldn't hold it together if I did. I'd already told Hermie what was going to happen. For weeks, he had looked at me as if asking me to make the decision. When I told the other dogs, one clearly said "the land of the angels," as if he understood.

> My husband and I wandered around, watching Hermie, wishing he were young again. Strangely, dogs barked all around us that afternoon—even from homes we didn't know had dogs. I sensed Jess, a dear dog now in spirit and one of Hermie's friends, had been visiting in the days leading up to this. I believe she came to guide him.
>
> When the vet arrived, she confirmed it was time. Hermie now had breathing issues on top of everything else. As we sat with him, he passed peacefully. In his final moment, he let out a sound—half bark, half howl. It was the same "welcome home" song he sang with Jess and Camper, another dog in spirit. Through my tears, I knew they had come to walk him home.
>
> Fifteen months later, we adopted another dachshund. He's nothing like Hermie, and that's okay. Hermie is still the photo on my phone. I'm nearly ready to change it—but not quite. And that's okay too.
>
> Being kind to ourselves in grief is as important as the love we give our pets.
>
> Wendy

Hiding your emotions or suppressing your grief can prolong the healing process. While it may feel like others don't understand, some people do—whether it's friends, family, or support groups who have experienced similar losses. Seeking out these connections can provide comfort and reassurance that you're not alone in your pain.

Grieving the loss of a pet can also stir emotions tied to previous losses, bringing back memories of the pets who came before. This is a natural part of the grieving process. Each pet we love leaves an indelible pawprint on our hearts, and their memories often become deeply intertwined. Allow yourself to acknowledge these feelings and permit yourself to mourn each loss—it's an important and healing step on your journey through grief.

In the following chapters, we will explore ways to cope with these feelings, find support, and honour the special bond you shared with your pet. Remember, your grief is a reflection of your love, and there is no timeline or right way to mourn. Allow yourself the grace to feel and heal in your own time.

Chapter 3

The Stages Of Grief In Pet Loss

Grieving the loss of your beloved pet is an intensely personal experience, but it often follows a pattern of emotional stages. While everyone processes grief differently, understanding these stages can help you navigate your emotions and find ways to heal. This chapter explores the five stages of grief as they relate to pet loss, offering insights, exercises, and journal prompts at the end of the chapter to support your journey.

Denial: "This Can't Be Real"

Denial often accompanies the initial shock of losing your pet. You may find yourself struggling to accept the reality of their absence. This stage can feel surreal; you keep staring at the door, expecting that they might walk back through the door any minute. You may catch yourself instinctively setting down their food bowl or waiting to hear their paws on the floor. These small habits can make the loss feel even more unreal.

Example Thought: "I woke up today, rolled over and you weren't there. For a moment, I thought you must have taken yourself outside. I snuggled deeper into the blankets, and then it hit me."

Denial serves as a buffer, giving your mind time to adjust to the painful reality.

Anger: "Why Did This Happen?"

Anger is a natural response to loss. You may feel frustrated toward circumstances, the vet, yourself, or even the universe for taking your pet away. This stage can also manifest as a deep sense of injustice—"They didn't deserve this."

It's essential to recognise that anger is a valid emotion, and it's okay to feel it. However, avoid letting it consume you or isolate you from others who want to support you.

Example Thought: "Why did this have to happen to my pet? They were so healthy and full of life—this is so unfair! Maybe they'd still be here if I had caught it sooner."

These kinds of thoughts reflect the frustration and sense of injustice that often accompany grief, especially when circumstances feel out of your control.

Bargaining: "And the What Ifs?"

In this stage of grief, you may find yourself replaying events and questioning whether you could have done something differently. This internal dialogue often leads to feelings of guilt and relentless "what ifs." You might think, "*What if I had noticed something was wrong sooner?*" or "*What if I had chosen a different treatment or gotten a second opinion?*" "*What if I had waited?*"

Example Thought: "If I had taken them to the vet earlier, maybe they would still be here. I should have seen the signs—this is my fault."

Bargaining often stems from our deep love and sense of responsibility for our pets. It's a way of trying to make sense of the loss, even if it means unfairly blaming yourself. While these thoughts are painful, they are a regular part of grieving. Recognising that you did the best you could with the knowledge and resources you had can help bring self-compassion to this stage.

Depression: "How Can I Go On Without Them?"

Depression can feel like an immense weight, making it challenging to engage with daily life. You might experience a profound emptiness, as if a part of you is missing. This stage often brings intense sadness, withdrawal from others, and a deep sense of hopelessness.

"I cancelled all my appointments because I just couldn't face another person. I felt like if they looked at me, they'd see right through me—see my broken heart and know I was a fraud, hiding behind a mask of strength."

I didn't want anyone to know how deeply I was struggling. I didn't want others to know that my grief was causing anxiety, sleepless nights, and even physical symptoms. I'd start shaking at sudden loud noises and often felt a heaviness, even sharp pains, in my heart. I wouldn't have considered myself someone who lacked strength, but this feeling was consuming me, and I didn't know how to handle it in a healthy way.

Grieving the loss of a pet can also bring up unresolved emotions from past losses, compounding the pain. If your pet's death was sudden, you might feel even more disoriented and lost. Many of my clients share that they didn't realise how deeply their pet's passing would resurface grief from years ago—whether it was another beloved pet, a person they lost, or even a loss of connection to themselves.

Acceptance: "Finding Peace in the Memories"

Acceptance doesn't mean forgetting or no longer feeling sadness. Instead, it's about finding a way to carry your pet's love with you while embracing the joy they brought to your life. This stage is about honouring their memory while allowing yourself to heal.

You may find comfort in small things—one of their favourite toys, a special photo, or even a quiet moment of reflection. Acceptance is about recognising that while life will never be the same, it can still be beautiful.

Moving Forward with Compassion

Grief is not a linear process; you may find yourself revisiting these stages multiple times. That's okay. Be gentle with yourself as you navigate this journey. Each stage is a step toward healing, and every emotion is a testament to the depth of love you shared with your pet. Remember, you are not alone, and seeking support as you move through this process is okay.

Denial Exercise:
- Allow yourself to acknowledge the reality of your loss gently. Write down a memory of your pet that brings you comfort. Revisit this memory whenever denial feels overwhelming.

Journal Prompt:
- What was the first thing you loved about your pet when they entered your life? Write about that moment and how it made you feel.

Anger Exercise:
- Channel your anger into movement. Take a walk, do a gentle workout, or punch a pillow if that feels cathartic. Go for a swim and scream underwater. Physical activity helps release the built-up tension that anger creates in your body. While you might not feel like exercising, even small movements can release endorphins, which naturally help reduce anger and improve your mood.

Journal Prompt:
- Write a letter to your pet expressing all your emotions, including your anger. Let it all out, knowing your pet's love for you was unconditional.

Bargaining Exercise:
- Remind yourself: No matter what happened, you made the best decisions you could with the information and resources you had at the time. You acted out of love and care, which your pet felt throughout their life.

Journal Prompt:
- What are some ways your pet brought you joy? List moments where you knew they were truly happy and loved.
- Write down three things you did to give your pet a happy and loving life.

Depression Exercise:
- **Create a Sacred Space:** Find a quiet area where you can sit and allow yourself to feel whatever emotions arise. Bring along a journal or a simple notepad—it doesn't have to be anything fancy. Let yourself write freely, letting your thoughts flow without judgment. Tears may come, and that's okay. This is a safe space for release. Remember, no one but you needs to see this, it's for your healing. If it feels right, you can even tear up your writing afterwards and release it to the wind, symbolising that your thoughts and emotions are now free, carried away like the breeze.

- **Connect with Your Pet in Spirit:** Light a candle and place a photo or memento of your pet nearby. Set aside a time each day to talk to them in spirit. Trust that your pet is listening and supporting you during these moments. These small rituals of connection can offer comfort and a sense of closeness, even in the darkest times.

Journal Prompt
- **Reflect on how your pet changed your life.** What lessons did they teach you? In what ways did they make you a better person?

Acceptance Exercise:
- Create a tribute to your pet, for example, a scrapbook, a photo album, or plant a tree in their honour. Engaging in a meaningful activity can help you channel your grief into something beautiful.

Journal Prompt:
- Write about your favourite memory with your pet. How does it feel to relive that moment? What emotions does it bring up?

"There is nothing to forgive — only love remains, and it wraps around us both."

Chapter 4

Coping With Guilt After Pet Loss

Guilt is one of the most common emotions people experience after losing a beloved pet. It often stems from our deep bond with our animals and our desire to do everything possible for them. This chapter will help you understand guilt as a natural response to loss, address the persistent "what if" questions, and guide you toward self-forgiveness and healing.

Understanding Guilt as a Natural Response

Guilt often arises because of the immense love we have for our pets. When they pass, we feel responsible, even when we've done everything we can to care for them. It's essential to recognise that guilt is a natural part of the grieving process—it's your heart's way of grappling with the pain of loss and the desire to have done more for your cherished companion.

In my sessions, I hear the "what if" question over and over. *"What if I gave my pet some more time? What if I had been home? What if I didn't do this or didn't do that?"* These questions weigh heavily on the heart, but sadly, we can't change what has happened. Beating ourselves up over a decision isn't going to bring back our pet. I wish it would—most of us would give anything for one more day or even just one more cuddle.

At times like this, be kind to yourself, and remember you did the best you could. Your pet knows you acted with love and kindness. They saw your care, and that is what mattered most to them.

 The U-Turn That Changed My Life

I was so excited—I had just bought a new home on the Sunshine Coast. The drive down took nearly 18 hours, and the car was packed so tightly that there was barely any room for the dogs. But we didn't mind; we were all eager for this fresh start, this new chapter we would share.

My two dogs and I settled quickly into the new house, even though most of our furniture hadn't arrived yet. The following day, I emptied the car and set up what little we had. I had been busy all day, and as it got late, I realised I needed food. So, we all jumped in the car and headed out.

Driving along the motorway, I suddenly realised I was going the wrong way. Without thinking, I made a quick U-turn, then, in an instant, everything went dark.

When I woke up, I was in hospital. My car was completely written off. I was in a bad state and confined to a wheelchair. Worst of all, both my beloved dogs had passed in the accident. My life would never be the same again.

> I tortured myself with every "what if" imaginable. All I wanted was for my two beautiful dogs to come back to me. I was consumed by grief, unable to forgive myself for what had happened. They didn't deserve this, and I was certain I would never, ever be able to forgive myself.
>
> My body was battered and broken, and being in a wheelchair felt like some punishment for what I had done. I tried counselling, I tried every holistic treatment I could find—but nothing eased the pain. Then, someone suggested I try animal communication. In desperation, I made a booking.
>
> We had two sessions. In the first session, Donna gave me simple steps for 30 days. A month later, we met again, and what happened next can only be described as a miracle. Yes, I had to do the inner work, but through those sessions, I was finally able to forgive myself, knowing, without a doubt, that my dogs were okay. I was able to stop all the "what if" questions that I had been playing in my head ever since the accident.

Addressing Common "What If" Questions

It's natural to replay events and second-guess decisions, especially when the outcome is not what you hoped for. The "what if" questions are part of processing the loss, but dwelling on them can become a heavy burden.

- "What if I had noticed the signs sooner?" Response: You acted with the knowledge and resources you had at the time. Hindsight may give clarity, but judging yourself for decisions made in the moment with love is unfair.

- "What if I made the wrong decision about euthanasia?" Response: Choosing to ease your pet's suffering is one of the hardest and most selfless acts of love. It's a decision made with their comfort, dignity, and quality of life in mind, even when it breaks your heart.

- "What if I wasn't there when they passed?" Response: Your pet knew your love every single day. The bond you shared doesn't diminish because you weren't physically present at the moment of their passing. They know if you could have been with them, you would have.

Your pet may have passed without you present, as they knew it would be difficult for you to see them as they are passing. Know, they'll always carry your love with them.

 Please Forgive Me

I had to make that call today—the one I never wanted to make. I had hoped you would pass peacefully, with me holding your paw, surrounded by love and comfort. I couldn't bear to see you in pain any longer. Please forgive me. I made the decision with a heavy heart, believing it was the most compassionate choice for you. It wasn't something I took lightly. I asked for strength and forgiveness because, deep down, I didn't feel equipped to make that choice on your behalf.

Watching you suffer was unbearable. I felt so powerless, knowing there was nothing more I could do to ease your pain. I just wanted to do what was best for you, even though it broke my heart.

Euthanasia—the decision to gently end a pet's life to relieve pain and suffering—is often made out of deep love and compassion. While it can bring peace to a suffering animal, it can also leave pet guardians grappling with a wave of difficult emotions, including guilt, sorrow, and self-doubt. If you've recently had to make this heartbreaking choice, know that these feelings are a natural part of the grieving process. Forgiving yourself is not only important—it's essential for healing.

> **Fergie**
>
> When I made the call to euthanise my senior boy Fergie, this brought a whole new set of mixed emotions. I found myself questioning if it was truly the right time, or if there was something more I could have done. Even when you know in your heart it was the most selfless act to end their suffering, the feelings of guilt, doubt, and responsibility can linger.

I can't count the number of times people have shared with me their hope that their beloved pet would pass away peacefully in their sleep. It's a wish we all hold onto. But the reality is, more often than not, we are the ones who must lovingly guide our pets through their final moments. Studies estimate that around 41% of pets, particularly those with age-related or degenerative conditions, pass with the help of euthanasia. While this number may vary between countries and regions, it's clear that choosing euthanasia is a common and often necessary act of love to ensure a gentle and dignified goodbye.

Forgiving Yourself for Difficult Decisions

Forgiveness is a crucial step in coping with guilt. Many pet parents struggle with forgiving themselves for decisions they made during their pet's life or at the end of it. Please remember, the choices you made were driven by love, even if they were tough choices to make.

To begin forgiving yourself:

- Acknowledge your emotions: Feeling guilt, sadness, or regret is okay. These feelings reflect the depth of your love.

- Reframe your perspective: Instead of focusing on what you perceive as mistakes, remind yourself of how you cared for and loved your pet.

- Talk to your pet in spirit: Share your feelings with them. Imagine them responding with the unconditional love they always showed you.

Transforming Guilt into a Tribute of Love

Rather than allowing guilt to consume you, channel it into honouring your pet's memory. Your love for them can inspire acts of kindness and healing.

- **Create a memorial:** Dedicate a space in your home to celebrate their life, and place all their favourite items in this area. Consider creating a coffee table book of beautiful photos that bring back memories of the love and joy you shared. Pop the book in a place where you are reminded of your love and can reflect on the time you spent together. If creating a photo book seems too hard, print some photos and pop them in a little album in a handy place to access.

- **Volunteer or donate:** Support an animal rescue organisation or shelter in your pet's name. There are so many dog and cat rescues, and these pets need love and attention. Volunteer for a day or an afternoon, whenever you can spare some time, to enrich the lives of these pets. Many of my dogs came from local rescues, where I often foster dogs. I am what they call a foster fail. (Foster Fail - Someone who decides they can't live without the pet they have fostered).

  Whilst you may not be ready to adopt another pet, being able to go and walk and sprinkle some love on a pet in rescue can help with the grieving process.

- **Share their story:** Write about your pet and the joy they brought to your life. Sharing your experience can help others who are grieving.

To My Sweet Misti Girl,

My beautiful, sweet girl, how do I even begin to thank you for nearly 16 years of pure love? You have shown me the true essence of patience, loyalty, and unconditional love. You have taught me to cherish what matters. You were my everything, you are a part of my heart, my reason for getting up every morning. You taught me the meaning of patience, loyalty, and the kind of love that never asks for anything in return.

You showed me what really matters in life—to live in the moment and cherish everything. To smell the flowers and breeze, to appreciate the small blessings, and to greet each day with wonder and gratitude. You were a living reminder to embrace each day as if it were our last, to be grateful for every blessing, no matter how small. Through your eyes, I learned to see the world with wonder and joy, and through your heart, I understood the boundless capacity for love.

You weren't just a pet—you were a part of my soul, a piece of my heart, and the light in my life. You gave me more than I could ever give back, and even now, your love continues to guide me.

As I prepare to say goodbye, I know you know how deeply I loved you and what you meant to me. I will carry your love forever in my heart until the day we meet up again.

You will always be with me, my sweet girl. I love you more than words can ever say.

Forever and always,
Your Mommy

Goodbye Chance

You'll Be Fine in the Morning- I never saw the silver creeping through your fur or how the light in your eyes softened over time. I didn't notice how your steps grew slower, each taking just a little more effort.

I missed the quiet signs, the way you'd pause a little longer to rest, or how you would lower your head with a gentleness that seemed new. Then, one day, I realised how much it took for you to lift your head, how your breath was lighter, a soft whisper I hadn't been listening for.

A tear rolled down my cheek. "I'm not ready, Channy," I whispered. "I don't have enough photos … there are still so many adventures. I don't want to wake up and find you gone. It's too soon."

I placed my head against yours and whispered, "I don't want to say Goodbye. I can't … but I know I have to. Not for me, but for you."

Let's go back to where it all began, I thought. I'll tell you about your adoption day, and as I cradle you close, I'll retell your story from the beginning—the way you came into my life and changed it, one beautiful memory at a time.

Nadia

Exercise: Releasing Guilt

Take a few moments to sit quietly and reflect on your feelings. Write a letter to your pet, expressing your love, your regrets, and your gratitude. End the letter by thanking them for the joy they brought into your life and imagining them sending you love in return.

A letter to a good boy … Today marks 6 months since you've been gone. It hasn't gotten easier, only harder, as the days fall into weeks and weeks into months. I miss you, buddy. It feels like we were together just yesterday, but it's been 6 months without my best buddy, my best friend. I thought I would stop crying at night, I haven't. I know you understand how hard it's been without you.

I am grateful for all the times we had together. The crazy things you did whilst we were in the car, the way you used to fart, to make me laugh. The way you snuggled me when you knew I was hurting.

I hated being alone. I found another dog called Kevin at the rescue where you came from. He looks just like you. Although he is nothing like you, he makes me laugh and is a good boy. I MISS YOU, my boy. I miss you so much, it still hurts every day. I thought I would see you in my dreams, but I haven't. I want you to know that Kevin isn't there to replace you, but to comfort me. I miss you, my big love bug. And I can't stand this pain in my heart, I miss you so much, I love you, and I hope you are watching over me. Until we meet again.

Journal Prompt

- What are three ways you showed your pet love and care during their life? Reflect on these moments and how they demonstrate your devotion.
- If your pet could speak to you now, what would they say about the love and care you gave them?

Moving Toward Healing

Guilt reflects love; it's not meant to overshadow the joy and connection you shared with your pet. Be gentle with yourself and remember that your pet's love for you was unconditional. By forgiving yourself and celebrating their memory, you can begin to transform guilt into a lasting tribute to the bond you shared.

Chapter 5

Dealing With Blame And Forgiving Yourself

When a beloved pet leaves this world, it's not just grief that moves in—the quiet shadow of blame often takes root. You might find yourself replaying moments, scrutinising decisions, and wishing for one more chance to do things differently. These thoughts aren't a reflection of failure; they're proof of how deeply you loved and committed to your pet's happiness and well-being.

Blame can feel like a loop—a relentless stream of "What if I had…?" or "Why didn't I…?" Even the most devoted pet parents aren't immune. Whether second-guessing a decision at the vet, questioning missed signs of illness, or regretting time away, this internal dialogue is driven by the same love that made your bond so special.

It's important to understand that blame is often our mind's desperate attempt to make sense of loss. As caregivers, we hold ourselves to impossibly high standards, carrying the weight of perfection in a world where life is anything but predictable. We want to believe we could have done more. We want to believe that maybe, just maybe, we could have changed the ending.

But love doesn't mean having all the answers. It means showing up—imperfectly, wholeheartedly, with the best intentions you had in each moment.

So let's begin the healing.

Take a breath. Place your hand over your heart. And remember: You did the best you could with the knowledge, energy, and resources you had at the time. That truth matters.

Letting go of blame doesn't mean forgetting. It means releasing the illusion that you had control over every outcome. It means choosing to see the entire picture—the joy, care, and little moments of connection your pet felt daily.

Reflecting with hindsight makes it easy to wish we had done something differently. But hindsight has a cruel way of showing us clarity we didn't have in the moment. You were navigating complex, emotional terrain and acted from a place of deep love.

Forgiveness is the doorway to freedom.

It begins with the self. Not because you did something wrong, but because you deserve peace.

Try speaking these words aloud, or writing them down when the guilt feels heavy:

- "I did the best I could with the information I had."
- "My pet knows I loved them and always wanted the best for them."

- "I am human, and it's okay to grieve, question, and forgive."

And if your heart still carries blame directed outward—to a vet, a friend, a family member—know this: forgiveness is not about excusing harm. It's about releasing your soul from the grip of resentment. It's about reclaiming your emotional energy so that love, not anger, has the final word.

One powerful shift can change everything as you move through this: transforming blame into gratitude.

Gratitude doesn't erase the pain. It simply allows light to enter the cracks.

Instead of staying tethered to what went wrong, let yourself remember the good—the tail wags, the soft purrs, the way they knew just when you needed them close. Let your grief sit beside your gratitude. They can co-exist, gently, like old friends.

And when you're ready, here's a sacred practice to support your healing ...

A Heart-Healing Ritual: Writing Th ough Blame and Into Grace

1. **Write a Letter to Yourself** - Let it all out. The blame. The guilt. The "what ifs." Let your heart speak without censoring or editing. Be honest. Be raw. Be you.

2. **Acknowledge the Love** - In the same letter, remind yourself of the love and care you gave your pet. List specific examples—how you comforted them when they were scared, how you played their favourite games, or how you made their final moments as peaceful as possible.

3. **Hear Their Voice** - Now, shift the voice. Imagine your pet speaking to you. What would they say? Perhaps:

   "Thank you for loving me. Thank you for doing your best. You didn't fail me—you walked beside me until the very end."

   Write their words as if they were sitting right next to you.

4. **Let it Go** - When the time feels right, release the letter. Burn it. Bury it. Or tuck it into a special keepsake box. Choose a ritual that symbolises letting go—not of their memory, but of the blame holding your heart hostage.

5. **Anchor in Gratitude** - Write a new letter. This time, focus on what you're thankful for. Thank your pet for the joy, the lessons, and the companionship. And thank yourself for showing up, loving so deeply, and continuing to heal.

 Letter To Spyro

I don't even know where to begin, because my heart still aches with the shock of losing you so quickly. One minute you were purring beside me, and the next I was being told you were sick—really sick—and it all happened so fast that I barely had time to understand, let alone say goodbye. I keep asking myself how I didn't see it coming. How did I not notice that something was wrong? You were hiding this from me, trying to protect me. That thought breaks me even more, because I would have done anything to protect you.

I feel so much guilt, I wish I had done things differently. I wish I had taken more time off work to be by your side in the last few days. I hated leaving you, even for a short amount of time. The night we went out to dinner, I was torn in half. I watched you try to climb the stairs to get to me, your little body still determined to be close, even through the pain. I wasn't there the way I wanted to be. I feel like I let you down. I know you needed me, and I tried, I really did … but it just never felt like enough.

The day I made the call to the vet was one of the hardest moments of my life. I was desperate to stop your pain, but I also wanted time to freeze. I needed more time with you, more cuddles, more words whispered in your ear. I hated that I couldn't take away your pain, that I couldn't do more. Even putting you in the car felt impossible—I didn't want to make things worse. So I waited for the vet to come to us, counting down the minutes while dreading every one that passed. I didn't want you to go. Not yet. Not ever.

There are so many "what ifs" that haunt me. What if I had noticed sooner? What if I had taken you to the vet a week earlier? What if I had never left your side for even a second? Would it have changed anything? Would you still be here? These questions swirl around endlessly in my mind, and I know they don't have answers, but I ask them anyway. I would give anything to rewind time, just to hold you in my arms again, to listen to your purr and tell you all the things I didn't get to say.

I want you to know how deeply I loved you. You were my heart, my companion, my shadow. I know you felt that love, even in those final days. I miss you so much it hurts. And if love could have saved you, you would have lived forever.
Mum

Walking Forward with Compassion

Blame may show up on this journey, but it doesn't have to stay. By recognising its source, loosening its grip, and welcoming in forgiveness, you begin to reclaim your light. Each step you take, no matter how shaky, reflects the fierce love you shared and the courage it takes to heal.

You are not alone. And you are not broken. You are walking a sacred path of grief—beneath it all, the bond remains, unshaken, eternal.

Your time to forgive, love, and rise again is now.

Chapter 6

Steps To Process And Heal From Grief

Rituals can provide a sense of closure and a meaningful way to celebrate your pet's life.

In a later chapter, I'll explore rituals and ceremonies in more depth. For some people, holding a formal ceremony for their pet after their passing might feel overwhelming or too emotional to consider. A simple closing ritual, such as lighting a candle and saying a few words in their memory, can be just as powerful.

Journaling and Reflecting on Memories

Journaling can be a deeply healing tool during the grieving process after losing a beloved pet. It provides a safe and private space to express emotions, process memories, and work through the complex layers of grief. Writing allows you to slow down and truly feel what's coming up, which can be difficult to do in the hustle of daily life. Sometimes, simply putting thoughts into words—whether it's a flood of sadness, cherished memories, or even feelings of anger or guilt, can be incredibly cathartic.

You don't need a fancy notebook or special tools to get started. If you have a beautiful journal and colorful pens, wonderful! But a plain notepad or even scraps of paper work just as well. The act of writing is what's important, not how it looks. It's about creating a space where your emotions can flow freely without judgement.

That said, journaling isn't for everyone, at least not in the traditional sense. One client I spoke with shared that the thought of sitting down to write felt overwhelming. She said, "I just can't make myself do it, it feels too much right now." For her, recording her thoughts on her phone felt much more manageable. She found comfort in speaking her feelings aloud and saving them as voice notes to revisit later.

There's no right or wrong way to journal. Whether you write, type, or record your voice, the key is to find what feels natural to you. Journaling, in any form, allows you to honour your grief, reflect on your journey, and, over time, begin to heal. Sometimes, even the smallest act of sharing your thoughts, on paper or through spoken words, can make a big difference.

Below are 10 journal prompts designed to help you reflect and heal:

1. What happened, and how did it make you feel?
2. Describe the first time you met your pet. What were your initial thoughts and emotions?
3. What was a small, everyday routine you shared with your pet that you now miss the most?
4. Write about a time when your pet comforted you during a difficult moment. How did they help you?

5. Reflect on a holiday or special occasion you spent with your pet. What made it memorable?

6. Write a letter to your pet thanking them for all the joy and love they brought into your life.

7. Describe your pet's favorite spot in the house or yard. What made it special to them?

8. Write about a lesson your pet taught you—whether it was about love, patience, or something else entirely.

9. Imagine your pet could talk to you now. What do you think they would say to comfort you?

10. Create a list of your pet's unique quirks and habits that made them so special to you.

These prompts can help you focus on the love and happiness your pet brought into your life, providing solace during your healing process.

Finding a Support Community

Grieving the loss of a pet can feel isolating, but you are not alone. Finding a support community can be a vital part of your healing journey. Consider reaching out to:

- Breed-Specific Groups: If your pet was a Golden Retriever, Pug, or another specific breed, there are often online and local communities dedicated to these breeds. These groups can provide understanding and shared experiences.

- Rescue or Shelter Groups: If your pet came from a rescue or shelter, connect with their community. Many rescues offer support for adopters who have lost their beloved pets.

- Pet Loss Support Groups: Look for local or virtual support groups dedicated to grieving pet owners. Sharing your feelings with others who understand can be incredibly comforting.

By connecting with others who have experienced similar losses, you may find solace and strength in their shared compassion and support. Grieving is not something you have to do alone; a community can help guide you through the healing process.

 Joey's passing - Setting my best friend free

I was gifted Joey, a one-and-a-half-year-old Labrador, by a friend who was returning to live in Germany and couldn't take him with her. Things were a little awkward at first—I felt like I was looking after someone else's baby and didn't know what I was doing. I had always dreamed of having a dog, but in my mind, it was a short-haired border collie with blue eyes.

But as time passed, Joey and I became incredibly close. He came everywhere with me and became my very best friend. We were like two peas in a pod. My daughter once said, "I think you love Joey more than me!" I quickly replied, "It's just a different kind of love!" (Quick-thinking mum moment!)

When Joey was nine, he was diagnosed with a tumour in his left eye. The specialist told me he'd never seen a growth like it in his 30 years of practice. Joey wasn't in any pain at the time, but we were told that if his eye started to squint, we'd need to remove it.

As you can imagine, I was devastated. I told myself, "He's had a good life—anything we get from here on is a bonus." But every time I thought about life without Joey, I cried. (Not in front of him or anyone else, of course—I'm a strong, independent woman!)

I found a holistic vet who treated Joey with acupuncture, Chinese herbs, and other natural therapies. To everyone's surprise, Joey went on to live a very full and happy life, with both of his eyes, and passed away at the ripe old age of 16. That might sound like a happy ending, but letting him go was a new life lesson.

Joey had slowed down in those final months. He would still go on short walks, but didn't run anymore. I had a ramp so he could still get in the car with me, but even then, he wasn't keen on coming on trips. He seemed to prefer staying home, which made me sad. He was still having hydrotherapy, monthly acupuncture, and all the lotions and potions I could give him to keep him going.

One day, I was chatting with someone and asked, "How do you know when it's time to let them go?" He replied, "You'll know when the time is right." That answer made me angry. I had never put an animal to sleep before, and I thought, *How are you supposed to know when it's the right time to say goodbye to your best friend?*

I hoped I'd kiss Joey goodnight and find he'd peacefully passed in his sleep, curled up in his bed the next morning. But that didn't happen. And, as it turns out, that man was right. One day, I just knew. The time had come.

I rang my friend and life coach, and we had a deep conversation over the phone (which I highly recommend). We talked about setting Joey free. We reflected on the 14 beautiful years we'd spent together and made a plan for what I needed to do.

I called my vet, who kindly offered to come to the house the following day. I also rang the crematorium and booked a time for them to arrive after the vet. I phoned my kids, and we all took Joey to his favourite place—Stumers Creek Dog Beach—for one last visit.

When the vet arrived, Joey was lying on his bed. He didn't get up. The whole family was there, sitting with him. The vet asked, "Are you ready?" And of course, no one's ever really ready. I leaned down, held Joey in my arms, and told him how much I loved him. I told him he had been the best dog in the whole wide world.

And then he was gone.

I had Joey cremated, and his ashes have sat on my bedside table for the last four years. I had planned to scatter them at all the places we'd lived together, but I'm not ready yet. I trust that when the time is right, I'll know.

After Joey passed, I couldn't believe how good I felt. It was such an odd feeling that it made me feel a little guilty. I wondered, *Why am I not crying for days and weeks? Am I cold-hearted?* But deep down, I think it had everything to do with that counselling session beforehand. It gave me peace. It helped me prepare my heart.

Gone but not forgotten.
Luv, Mum

"Some souls come into our lives and leave paw prints on our hearts—forever part of our journey."

Chapter 7

Helping A Pet Cope With The Loss Of Another Pet

I'm often asked, "Do pets grieve the loss of another pet in the family?"

The answer is a resounding yes.

Like us, animals form deep emotional bonds with their companions, and just like us, they grieve—each in their unique way. Understanding this shared experience can help pet owners feel less alone in their grief.

Some pets accept the change and move on fairly quickly. Others, however, may show signs of distress—withdrawal, loss of appetite, low energy, or a sudden disinterest in their usual activities. Some become hypervigilant, over-groom, or even act out with aggression. I've known dogs who suddenly started peeing inside the house, as if their grief disrupted their routine and sense of stability.

Others may become particularly clingy, following you from room to room or lying for hours in their departed friend's favourite sleeping spot. It's also important to remember: while your pet is grieving the loss of their companion, they're also picking up on your grief. Animals are deeply intuitive. They want to comfort us, but often don't know how. If their companion was the leader or the nurturing one in your home, your surviving pet might now feel unsure or overwhelmed by a role they don't know how to fill.

Be gentle with them. Give them space and time. You're both learning to live with this new 'normal' without your beloved pet.

At the Time of Passing

Whenever possible, include your surviving pet during their companion's final moments—whether at home or the vet clinic. Pets sense and understand death, and being present allows them to process the loss naturally, in a grounded way.

If euthanasia is planned, ask your vet if your pet can be in the room. You may be surprised at how calmly they accept the process. Often, they understand far more than we realise.

If your surviving pet wasn't present at the time of passing, allow them to see and smell the body afterwards. This helps them understand that their friend has transitioned, rather than "disappeared."

Allowing pets to say goodbye in their own way, helps with their grief process. They're less likely to search the house for their missing friend or show signs of confusion about the loss.

After Spyro passed, I wrapped him up and gently brought him downstairs so the dogs could say goodbye. Being senior dogs, they couldn't get upstairs to be part of his final moments. One by one, they approached the basket, leaned in to sniff him, and stood quietly. Each in their own silent, sacred farewell. It was humbling. It was beautiful.

And it reminded me how deeply animals feel.

7 Gentle Ways to Support a Grieving Pet

1. **Maintain routine** - Structure brings comfort. Stick to regular meal times, walks, play, and bedtime. Familiar rhythms provide a sense of safety during uncertain times, empowering you to provide stability in your pet's life.

2. **Provide Comfort** - Offer extra love, patience, and reassurance. Sit with them. Talk to them softly. If, in those quiet moments, the tears come, that's ok, this time together can be healing for both of you.

   I often recommend Australian Bush Flower Essence – Transition during times of loss. This blend supports both animals and humans through life-altering changes.

   - *For pets:* apply 7 drops along their spine, morning and night, for 14 days.
   - *For humans:* take 7 drops under the tongue.

   (Note: This remedy contains alcohol, so it's best applied topically for pets who may dislike the taste.)

   You can find it on the Australian Bush Flower Essences website or in most health food stores.

   Another gentle and widely available option is Bach Rescue Remedy—a natural blend of six flower essences that eases shock, stress, and emotional overwhelm. It's suitable for both pets and people. Follow the label's dosage for safe use.

3. **Offer Enrichment** - Engage their mind and senses. A snuffle mat is an excellent tool for treat-motivated dogs. Hide small treats inside and supervise as they sniff them out—a calming form of mental stimulation that helps release nervous energy. Remove the mat after each session to keep it special.

4. **Get Outside Together** - Fresh air, sunlight, and new smells are incredibly therapeutic. Take slow, relaxed walks—even short ones. Try new routes when your pet is ready, and let them sniff to their heart's content. For dogs, sniffing is like therapy—it helps them process the world around them.

5. **Consider a New Companion (With Care)** - A new pet can eventually bring joy back into your home, but timing and compatibility matter.

   If your surviving pet is elderly, unwell, or very attached to the one who passed, a new companion could cause more stress than comfort. Trust your intuition. Ask yourself: Is this for them—or for me?

6. **Seek Professional Support** - If your pet's grief feels prolonged or intense, reach out to your vet or a trusted animal behaviourist. Grief can impact health, and your pet deserves the chance to heal fully, not silently suffer. Seeking professional support can provide reassurance and guidance in this difficult time.

   And don't forget to care for yourself, too. Your pet will mirror your emotional state, so your healing is also theirs.

7. **Be Aware of Changing Dynamics** - In multi-pet homes, the loss of one can shift the social dynamic. You might notice mood changes or even a reshuffling of leadership roles. Allow them time to adjust, but step in gently if you sense tension or distress.

Supporting a grieving pet is an act of deep love. It's about walking through the heartache together—one gentle step at a time.

With kindness, patience, and presence, healing will return to both of you.

Chapter 8

How Do I Explain My Grief To Friends & Family?

When you lose a beloved pet, you lose more than just an animal companion—you lose a piece of your heart, a source of unconditional love, and often, your closest confidant. Explaining the depth of that loss to friends and family can feel isolating, especially when society doesn't always view pet grief with the same gravity as the loss of a human loved one.

This chapter explores how to help others understand your grief, respond to dismissive remarks, educate loved ones about the depth of pet loss, and set boundaries to protect your healing journey.

Helping Others Understand Your Bond

One of the hardest parts of grieving a pet is helping those around you understand the significance of your loss. For many people, a pet isn't "just a pet"—they are family. Pets offer companionship, joy, and comfort. They are a part of your daily life and routines, often filling a role no one else can.

I talk to grieving pet parents every day in my sessions, and I see firsthand the depth of love and pain they experience. People cry, share messages of love, and laugh when they remember their pet's quirks or hear messages I share from their pets in spirit. Despite witnessing this deep connection daily, when my own Golden Retriever, Ajax, passed away, I struggled to explain my pain to others.

Ajax was my soul mate, my confidant, and my rock. He stood by me during some of the darkest times of my life, including my battle with breast cancer. He made me laugh when I thought I'd never laugh again, and comforted me when I needed it most. He was more than a dog—he was the reason I found purpose in my work, helping others through their grief.

When Ajax passed, I initially received an outpouring of support. Friends sent flowers, messages, and kind words. But as time went on, I felt increasingly isolated. I stopped talking about him because I sensed people didn't understand. They didn't know the depth of our bond or what he meant to me. How could they? They only knew what they saw online or in passing.

I tried to explain to my father what Ajax had meant to me, but his response was, "It's just a dog." My father has never been someone deeply in touch with his emotions. I suppose it reflects his generation and the era he grew up in, where dogs were seen as animals kept outside, valued for their work rather than as companions. How could someone raised with this perspective possibly understand the depth of my bond with Ajax? It felt like an unbridgeable gap, one that left me feeling even more alone in my grief.

Responding to "It Was Just a Pet"

Hearing someone say, "It was just a cat or just a pet," can feel like a knife to the heart. Those words minimise your grief and suggest that your pain is invalid. While most people don't intend to hurt you with these remarks, their lack of understanding can still be deeply painful.

How to Respond:

1. **Stay Calm:** It's natural to feel defensive, but remember that their perspective comes from a place of misunderstanding, not malice.

2. **Educate Gently:** You might say, "I understand that not everyone feels the same about their pets, but for me, [pet's name] was a part of my family. Losing them has been incredibly hard."

3. **Protect Your Energy:** If you don't have the emotional bandwidth to explain, it's okay to change the subject or politely end the conversation.

For Those Close to You:

With loved ones, it can be helpful to share stories that illustrate the depth of your bond. For example, "Ajax wasn't just a dog. He was the one who comforted me when I was going through cancer. He brought me joy every single day. Losing him feels like losing a part of myself."

Educating Loved Ones on Pet Grief

Grief from losing a pet is just as valid as grief from losing a human loved one. However, society often fails to acknowledge this, making the experience feel even lonelier.

To help loved ones understand:

1. **Share Articles or Resources:** Many articles and books discuss the depth of pet grief. Sharing these can help others see your perspective.

2. **Please give them a copy of this book:** help them learn more about Pet Loss & Grief.

3. **Use Analogies:** Compare your loss to something they might understand, like losing a close friend, partner, or family member.

4. **Explain the Role of Your Pet:** Share how your pet impacted your daily life. For example, "Ajax wasn't just a dog. He was the reason I got up in the morning, the one who kept me grounded, and the source of so much joy and comfort in my life."

Setting Boundaries to Protect Your Healing

Grief is a personal journey, and it's okay to protect yourself from people or situations that make you feel worse. Setting boundaries can help you focus on your healing without feeling the need to justify your emotions.

Examples of Boundaries:

- **Limiting Conversations:** If someone dismisses your grief, it's okay to say, "I appreciate your concern, but I'd rather not talk about this right now."

  Sadly, much like my conversation with my father, I eventually gave up trying to explain my love for Ajax and how much he had meant to me. For 13 years, we walked through life together, and he had been so much more than "just a dog." He had been my everything. He was there through so many difficult times. Trying to convey that depth of connection to someone who couldn't see beyond the old notions of dogs as mere animals felt futile.

- **Avoiding Unsupportive People:** If certain friends or family members consistently belittle your feelings, consider spending less time with them while you heal.

- **Prioritising Your Needs:** Allow yourself to grieve in whatever way feels right, whether talking about your pet, creating a memorial, or taking time alone.

Navigating Isolation and Finding Support

When others don't understand your grief, it's easy to feel isolated. You might even begin to question whether your feelings are valid. In these moments, remember that your grief is a reflection of your love, and that love is worth honouring.

Find other like-minded people to talk with. There is nothing wrong with seeking the help of a professional grief counsellor who can provide a safe space to share your feelings.

Healing Th ough Shared Stories & Art

Sharing your pet's story can be a powerful way to process your grief and help others understand. Expressing your emotions can be deeply therapeutic through writing, talking, or creating art.

When I finally started sharing Ajax's story again, I found that people began to see the depth of my love and loss. I talked about how he supported me through cancer, how he made me laugh with his goofy antics, and how he always seemed to know when I needed comfort.

Art can also be a fun and deeply therapeutic way to process grief. You might like to create a clay sculpture of your pet or something symbolic that represents them. Painting or decorating a stone with your pet's name, paw prints, or other meaningful imagery can also be a beautiful way to process your grief.

Journal Prompts for Reflection

1. What made your pet unique? Write about their personality, quirks, and habits.

2. How did your pet impact your daily life?

3. What is your favourite memory with your pet?

4. How has your pet influenced the person you are today?

5. What do you wish others understood about your grief?

6. How can you honour your pet's memory in a way that feels meaningful to you?

7. What did your pet teach you about love and loyalty?

8. Who has been supportive during your grief journey, and how can you express gratitude to them?

9. What emotions come up when you think about your pet?

10. If your pet could send you a message from the afterlife, what would they say?

Final Thought

Explaining your grief to friends and family can be challenging, especially when society doesn't always recognise the depth of pet loss. But your grief is valid, and your love for your pet is a testament to the bond you shared. Be kind to yourself, set boundaries when needed, and remember that seeking support from those who genuinely understand is okay. Through sharing your story and honouring your pet's memory, you can begin to heal while keeping their spirit alive in your heart.

Chapter 9

Helping Children Cope With Pet Loss

When a beloved pet passes away, it's not just the adults in the family who feel the loss—children often experience profound grief as well. For many children, the death of a pet may be their first encounter with loss, making it a critical opportunity to guide them through understanding, processing, and coping with grief. This chapter provides compassionate strategies to help children navigate the loss of a pet, ensuring they feel supported and heard.

Explaining Death in an Age-Appropriate Way

Children's understanding of death varies greatly depending on their age, developmental stage, and prior experiences. It's important to tailor your explanation to their level of comprehension, while being honest and gentle.

Preschool-Aged Children (3-5 Years)

At this age, children may struggle to understand the permanence of death. They might believe their pet will return or think death is temporary. While it may feel easier to say, *"They were put to sleep,"* this phrase can unintentionally create fear or confusion, making children worry about what happens when they themselves *"go to sleep."* Instead, use simple, clear, and honest language to explain what has happened.

Instead of saying, *"Fluffy went to sleep,"* say, *"Fluffy's body has stopped working, and she won't be coming back."*

Avoid euphemisms that may confuse them, such as "gone away" or "put to sleep."

School-Aged Children (6-12 Years)

Children in this age group begin to understand the permanence of death. They may have more questions and feel sadness, confusion, or guilt.

Answer their questions honestly but with sensitivity. For example, if they ask, *"Why did Fluffy die?"* you might say, *"She was very old, and her body couldn't work anymore. [Pet's name] is not with us anymore, but we can still remember all the fun times we had with them. It's okay to be sad, and we can talk about how we miss them."*

Reassure them that nothing they said or did caused the pet's death.

In my sessions, I often talk with parents who are concerned about how they will explain their pet's illness and eventual passing to their children. I encourage them to have open conversations, take lots of photos, and involve the children in creating memories. Giving children choices is essential, such as whether they'd like to attend the pet's passing or participate in saying goodbye is essential.

Teenagers (13 and Older)

Teenagers are capable of a more mature understanding of death, but they may also suppress their feelings to appear strong. Encourage open conversations and validate their emotions.

Acknowledge their bond with the pet and remind them it's okay to grieve.

Be patient if they seem withdrawn or reluctant to talk; grief can manifest in different ways.

Helping Children Express Their Grief

Grief can feel overwhelming for children, especially if they lack the vocabulary or emotional tools to process their feelings. Providing outlets for expression can help them navigate their emotions.

Encourage Open Conversations

Create a safe space where your child feels comfortable sharing their feelings. Use prompts to help them articulate their grief:

"What do you miss most about Fluffy?"

"What's your favourite memory with her?"

Creative Outlets

Children often express their emotions through art, writing, or play. Encourage activities that allow them to channel their grief:

Drawing pictures of their pet.

Writing a letter or a story about their pet.

Encourage them to take pictures together, play dress up, or add their favourite toys.

Creating a scrapbook of photos and memories.

Physical Outlets

Sometimes, children need to release pent-up energy to process their emotions. Encourage activities like walking, playing outdoors, or participating in sports.

Creating Rituals and Memorials with Kids

Involving children in rituals and memorials can give them a sense of closure and help them honour their pet's memory. Refer to my chapter on Rituals and Ceremonies.

Holding a Pet Memorial Service

A simple ceremony can give children a structured way to say goodbye. Let them participate in planning the service, whether choosing a song, sharing a memory, or helping to bury their pet's ashes or favourite toy.

 Speedie's Passing

At 3 years of age, I gave my son a mini fox terrier. I wanted a dog that was small but robust for a young child. The moment he saw her, he screamed in delight, "Is this my dog"? He wanted to sleep with her, eat with her and be with her every waking moment. They were inseparable! Even as he grew older, the minute he got home from school, she would sit with him whilst he did homework. They would play football in the backyard. He was an only child, and she was his best friend.

Over the years, Speedie developed a heart condition, and the medication caused her to have bladder leakage, which affected her quality of life. One winter morning, she wasn't her usual self, so I called the vet and scheduled a check-up later that day. My son, who was 11 at the time, and I spent a beautiful day together with Speedie and our other dogs, cuddling on the lounge.

> I took her outside just before we left to go to the vet. She sniffed the air and looked around our yard—it was as if she knew something wasn't right. On the way to the vet, Speedie had a seizure in the car and passed out, leaving my son distressed as I drove. At the vet, they explained Speedie needed an immediate blood transfusion and that her prognosis was very poor.
>
> After discussing it with my son and the vet, we decided to help her cross the rainbow bridge. I wondered if it was too much for him to deal with at the time, watching the process of his best friend's passing. I gave him the choice to leave and sit in the car with our other dog, but he decided he needed to be there for her.
>
> It was a traumatic experience for both of us. My son had lost his best friend, and we returned home with only her collar. He cried and slept for days with the dog collar tied around his arm. He questioned life and my decision, grappling with his first experience of death. We talked about her often, printed out photos, and put them on the walls. When her urn came home, she was placed near the television so we could see her and talk to her every day. We never wanted to forget her, and we didn't want her to forget us.

In these situations, giving children a sense of participation and control is crucial. Letting them say goodbye, create memories, and be involved in decisions where appropriate can help them process the experience.

Supporting a Child's Emotional Well-Being

Grieving children need consistent support and reassurance as they process their loss.

Normalise Their Emotions

Reassure your child that their feelings are valid and normal. Let them know it's okay to feel sad, angry, or confused, and that these emotions may come and go.

Be a Role Model for Healthy Grieving

Children look to adults for cues on how to handle emotions. Show them it's okay to feel sad and cry, but also demonstrate that healing is possible.

Share your feelings: *"I feel really sad that Speedie isn't here anymore, but I'm so thankful for the time we had with her."*

Avoid suppressing your grief entirely, as children may feel they need to do the same.

Monitor for Signs of Complicated Grief

While most children process grief naturally over time, some may struggle more deeply. Keep an eye out for signs they may need additional support, such as:

Persistent sadness or withdrawal that interferes with daily activities.

Difficulty eating, sleeping, or concentrating.

Expressing feelings of guilt or responsibility for the pet's death.

If you notice these signs, consider contacting a counsellor or therapist experienced working with grieving children.

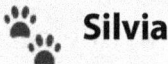 Silvia

Silvia, the cat, didn't always like our two little boys. She came to live with us after giving birth to four beautiful kittens at the RSPCA. She had 2 years of blissful peace with just my partner and me before our boys arrived. When they were small, she tolerated them, but she preferred adults. As the boys grew older and quieter, so did she. Soon she started to seek out their company, often curling up with them on the couch or in their beds. She liked to follow them outside and choose a sunny spot to curl up while they played on the trampoline. Her favourite place was a warm lap, and if you had the heated throw rug on, she was absolutely yours! The boys adored her, and she adored them - but if you missed the warning signs, she'd give you a little scratch to keep you on your toes!

When it was clear that Silvia was very sick, the boys were naturally very worried. Once her terminal diagnosis was in, it was time to have a difficult but heartfelt conversation with them about saying goodbye. At this stage, they were 8 and 10 years old, still small, but mature enough to be involved in honouring her in their way and saying goodbye to her if they wanted.

We made Silvia's last couple of weeks the most enjoyable we could. The boys had extra kitty snuggles and many photos, and made paw print impressions with polymer clay. We talked about how much she meant to them, and how they would like to remember her. Our 8 year old old loved her ringlet belly fluff, so we asked permission and cut some small pieces to pop in a special jar. We chose a special photo frame from the chemist.

When the day arrived to say goodbye to Silvia, the boys chose to attend school. They spent the afternoon with her, playing outside as she dozed on and off on the outdoor couch. Many cuddles were had, and lots of photos were taken. Before our vet Nina arrived, we asked again if the boys wanted to be with Silvia as she passed away. We talked about the process and what would happen. We were honest with them and explained that it would be sad and also peaceful. They both wanted to be with her and with us.

When our beautiful vet Nina arrived, she warmly explained what was going to happen in a way that the boys could understand. I held Silvia, and the boys sat next to me, all close enough to stroke her and to give her the love that she deserved in those final moments. The boys were incredibly brave, both quietly crying as Silvia peacefully slipped into a deep sleep and passed away. Our vet Nina left us to grieve with Silvia, together as a family. Once the initial wave of sadness had started to pass, we moved inside and tucked her into her favourite cat bed. We placed the cat bed on the end of our bed, so the boys could stroke her and talk to her. While heartbroken, they knew her energy had gone to a beautiful place, and she was no longer in so much pain.

In the morning, they both came in to see her. She looked so peaceful, all tucked up in her cat bed. They stroked her, shed some more tears, and knew this would be the last morning they would get to see her (in her physical body). I had organised for them to have time off school, so that they didn't have to rush their goodbyes and had time to feel sadness and grief.

When the lovely pet cremation owner, Tracey, arrived, she spent time reassuring the boys that she would take extra care of Silvia, just like she was her cat. She had brought a beautiful basket, blanket, and flowers for Silvia, and allowed the boys to say another goodbye. The boys were allowed to choose when they were ready to return to school, both decided to return the day after we collected Silvia's body.

We encouraged the boys to create a space in their rooms to remember Silvia. Our youngest chose to display the jar of belly fluff with the beautiful frame and picture that he chose. Our eldest chose a photo in a frame to go on his computer desk alongside a clay paw print. We encouraged them to share their feelings as the days grew into weeks and then into months. Around four months after Silvia's passing, the boys both agreed that their hearts had healed enough to welcome a new rescue into our family, and again, they were included in that process.

Two years have passed since Silvia left us, and they both talk about her regularly. Yes - there is still sadness and they both still miss her, but I'm confident that they will speak of their grief so we can tackle it together.

Exercise: Helping Children Remember and Heal

Here's a simple exercise to help children honour their pet while processing their emotions:

1. **Memory Jar**

   - Find a jar and decorate it with your child.

   - Invite your child to write down or draw their favourite memories with their pet on small pieces of paper.

   - Place the papers in the jar and keep it in a special place.

   - When your child feels sad, they can take out a memory to read or share.

2. **Family Storytelling Time**

   - Gather as a family and share favourite stories about the pet.

   - Encourage children to add stories or create imaginative stories about their pet's adventures in the afterlife.

   - This can help shift the focus to positive memories while fostering connection and healing.

A Compassionate Conclusion

Helping children cope with the loss of a pet requires patience, empathy, and understanding. By explaining death in an age-appropriate way, encouraging open expression, and creating meaningful rituals, you can provide them with the tools they need to process their grief. Remember, every child grieves differently, and there's no "right" timeline for healing. With your guidance and support, they can carry the love and lessons of their pet with them for a lifetime.

Chapter 10

Cremation vs Burying Your Pet

When your beloved pet passes, one of the most immediate and heart-wrenching decisions you'll face is what to do with their physical remains. This decision is often made during an incredibly emotional time, when grief is raw, and the idea of letting go feels unbearable. You are not alone in feeling this way. It's okay to feel overwhelmed, uncertain, or even conflicted about your options.

There's no "right" or "wrong" decision here—only what feels right for you and your pet. Every situation is unique, and sometimes circumstances like finances, living arrangements, or timing can dictate what's possible. What matters most is the love you shared and the care you're putting into honouring your pet, even now.

Considerations for Cremation

Cremation is a choice many pet parents make because it offers flexibility and allows them to keep their pet close physically. For some, it brings comfort knowing they can always carry a part of their pet with them.

1. Returning Ashes and Memorial Keepsakes

If you choose cremation, you may receive your pet's ashes in an urn or as part of a memorial keepsake. Some families display their pet's urn in a special place at home, while others prefer to keep it more private. I have a collection of urns and bamboo holders with precious ashes on my bookshelf. I had no idea what I wanted to do with Fergie's ashes, he hated being locked in a small space, so an urn just wasn't right for him, hence the decision was a bamboo holder.

Over the years, people have become so creative in what they can make with their pet's ashes. You might like to explore personalised options, such as turning ashes into jewellery, artwork or glass suncatchers. There are so many options available now for Keepsake jewellery. These keepsakes can help you feel connected to your pet's memory in a tangible way.

2. Places to Scatter Ashes

Scattering your pet's ashes in a meaningful location can be a beautiful and healing ritual. Think about the places your pet loved most—perhaps a favourite beach, garden, or walking trail. These special locations can become sacred spaces where you feel your pet's presence and remember the joy they brought into your life.

A little word of warning (and a funny one at that)—keep your mouth closed when releasing the ashes! The wind has a mischievous way of picking just the right moment to change direction, and you might end up with an unexpected taste of your pet's final journey. I can't help but laugh as I write this because it has happened to two of my friends. What started as a profoundly emotional moment quickly turned into one they will never forget—and one they still laugh about to this day.

3. Legal Guidelines for Scattering Ashes

Before scattering ashes, it's essential to check local laws and guidelines. While most private properties and outdoor spaces allow it, some public parks or nature reserves may have restrictions. Knowing what's permitted can help you plan this moment with care and confidence, and not worry about whether someone decides to interfere in your private moment.

Exploring Burial

Burial is a time-honoured way to say goodbye, offering a sense of permanence and connection to a specific place. For many, laying their pet to rest brings comfort and closure.

1. Home Burial Considerations

If you have the space and it's legally permitted, a home burial allows you to create a special resting place for your pet. You can mark the site with a tree, flowers, or a personalised marker, creating a physical space to visit and reflect. However, this choice can bring challenges if you ever need to move.

2. Pet Cemeteries: Choosing a Location and Planning Ahead

Pet cemeteries are another option, offering a professional resting place for your pet. Consider the cemetery's location, cost, and long-term management when exploring this route. One question I hear often is, "What happens if the cemetery closes?" This is a valid concern and something worth discussing with the cemetery operators before deciding.

3. Legal Restrictions and Environmental Factors

It's important to know the legal requirements for burial in your area. Urban or environmentally sensitive locations may have restrictions. Take time to ensure that your plans align with local guidelines and are safe for the environment.

4. What Happens If You Move?

One of the most common concerns about burial is the possibility of moving. Leaving your pet behind can feel heartbreaking, like you're leaving part of your soul. For some, exhuming and cremating their pet later is an option. It's not an easy decision, but it may bring closure and allow you to keep your beloved companion with you in a new form.

When Circumstances Dictate the Choice

You may feel limited by external factors—finances, living arrangements, or unexpected timing. I want you to know that these challenges do not diminish your love for your pet or the thoughtfulness you're bringing to this decision.

1. Financial Constraints and Available Options

Cremation is often more affordable than burial in a pet cemetery, but financial strain can make either option difficult. If you're unable to choose the option you would prefer, remember that your pet's love for you goes beyond these decisions. They wouldn't want you to feel guilt or regret.

2. Living in Apartments or Urban Areas

For those in apartments or urban areas, burial may not be possible. Cremation offers a practical and meaningful alternative, allowing you to keep your pet close in a way that works for your circumstances.

3. Making Peace with Difficul Situations

Sometimes, decisions must be made quickly, and you may feel uncertain about whether you made the "right" choice. In my sessions with pets in spirit, I'm reminded time and time again, they only care about the love and joy you shared during their life. Their soul has left, and they are free.

Messages from Pets in Spirit: Their Perspective on the Body

When I connect with pets in spirit, they often share a message of reassurance: they have no attachment to their body. Their soul is free, and they remain close to you in ways that transcend the physical.

Sometimes, guardians ask me, "What does my pet want?" The truth is, your pet doesn't want anything but your happiness. Rarely do they hold preferences about cremation or burial—they care only about the love in your heart and the thoughtfulness you're showing in making this decision.

Personal Reflections: Love Beyond the Urns

On my bookshelf, a gathering of urns and bamboo holders holds the remains of my cherished pets. Each one represents a life well-loved and a bond that remains unbroken. I often wonder what will happen to them when my own time comes.

To ensure my pets stay with me on my final journey, I've made a simple request—to be cremated along with their ashes and then planted with a tree, creating a space where life continues to grow. A place where dogs can sniff, roam, and discover my special tree, planted with love, and perhaps even leave their calling card as they take in the many scents surrounding it.

Making the Right Decision for You and Your Pet

Ultimately, the decision about cremation or burial is deeply personal. You might feel pressure to "get it right" or worry about what your pet would have wanted. Please let go of that worry, trust your instincts, honour your circumstances, and know that whatever choice you make comes from a place of love.

- Consider your emotional, financial, and practical needs.
- Take time to reflect on what feels right for you.
- Release guilt and focus on the love you shared.

Remember, your pet's soul is not tied to their physical remains. Their love for you transcends all of this, and they will always be with you, no matter what.

Chapter 11

Finding Joy And Purpose After Loss

Losing a beloved pet can leave an enormous void in your life, disrupting daily routines and altering your sense of purpose. But amidst the grief, there is an opportunity to rediscover joy, rebuild your life, and honour your pet's legacy meaningfully. This chapter explores how to navigate this delicate transition with compassion and intention.

Rebuilding Daily Routines

The absence of your pet can leave your days feeling unstructured and empty. Their presence was likely woven into the fabric of your daily life, from morning walks to evening cuddles. Rebuilding routines can provide a sense of stability and healing.

Suggestions:

- **Start Small:** Incorporate small, mindful activities into your day, like a morning stretch or an evening gratitude practice.

- **Fill the Gaps:** If you used to walk your pet at a specific time, consider taking a walk with a friend to maintain that familiar rhythm. If you prefer to go alone, try walking at a different time—this can give you the space to process your grief without unexpected conversations from those who may wish to ask about your pet before you're ready to share.

- **Create New Habits:** Use the time you once spent with your pet to try something new, like gardening, painting, volunteering, or a new sport.

Discovering New Sources of Joy

Grief can make joy feel unattainable, but small steps toward happiness are possible. Finding new sources of joy doesn't mean replacing your pet; nurturing your well-being while carrying their love with you.

Ideas to Explore:

- **Nature Therapy** Spend time in nature to reconnect with the world around you. A quiet walk in a park can be both soothing and inspiring.
- **Creative Outlets:** Channel your emotions into art, music, or writing. Creativity can be a powerful form of self-expression and healing.
- **Celebrate Small Wins:** Acknowledge even the smallest moments of happiness—a beautiful sunset, a kind word from a friend, or a moment of peace.

Exploring Personal Growth Through Grief

Grief is a transformative experience. While painful, it can also be an opportunity for deep personal growth and self-discovery. Reflecting on the lessons your pet taught you can help you find meaning in their loss.

Reflections for Growth:

- **Lessons Learned:** What did your pet teach you about love, patience, and resilience? Write these lessons down as a way to honour their impact on your life.
- **Strength Through Adversity:** Recognise your strength in facing this loss. Celebrate your ability to navigate one of life's hardest challenges.
- **Embrace Change:** Use this moment to explore areas of your life you'd like to grow in, whether building stronger relationships, developing new skills, or pursuing long-held dreams.

Exercises and Journal Prompts

1. Write about a moment when your pet brought you pure joy. How can you recreate or honour that feeling in your life now?
2. List three small changes you can make to your daily routine to bring comfort and stability.
3. Reflect on qualities your pet embodied (e.g., loyalty, playfulness). How can you embrace this quality in your own life?
4. Write a letter to your pet, sharing how you plan to honour their memory moving forward.
5. Brainstorm ways to give back to animals or people in your community. Which idea excites you the most, and why?
6. Create a "bucket list" of experiences or goals you'd like to pursue in honour of your pet.
7. Reflect on how your pet's love has shaped who you are today. What qualities in yourself are you proud of because of them?
8. Imagine your pet could see you now. What would they want for you? How can you take a step toward that vision?
9. Write about a hobby or activity you've always wanted to try. How can you start incorporating it into your life?
10. Think about your pet's favourite place or activity. How can you use that memory to create a new tradition or ritual?

By rebuilding your routines, seeking joy, helping others, and reflecting on personal growth, you can honour your pet's memory while rediscovering purpose and meaning in your life. Remember, healing takes time, and moving forward at your own pace is okay.

Chapter 12

How To Honour Your Pet's Memory

When a beloved pet passes away, finding meaningful ways to honour their memory can help ease the grief and ensure their presence remains a cherished part of your life. This chapter explores various ways to celebrate and honour your pet's life, from creating memorials and keepsakes to planting living tributes and keeping their spirit alive through rituals. Each act of remembrance is a step toward healing and maintaining the bond you shared.

Creating Memorials and Keepsakes

Creating a memorial for your pet can provide a tangible way to remember them. It gives you a dedicated space to reflect on their life and the joy they brought to yours. Memorials and keepsakes can take many forms, depending on what feels most meaningful to you.

- **A Special Place in Your Home**: Dedicate a corner or shelf in your home to your pet's memory. Include their photo, collar, or favourite toy alongside candles or flowers. This space can serve as a comforting reminder of their presence.

- **Personalised Keepsakes**: Many people find solace in creating or purchasing items commemorating their pet. This could be a piece of jewellery engraved with their name, a custom-made paw print mould, or a photo book filled with your favourite memories.

- **Memory Boxes**: A memory box is a fantastic way to keep treasured items related to your pet. Include items like their favourite leash, a lock of fur, or letters you've written to them.

- **Art and Portraits**: Commissioning a custom portrait of your pet or creating artwork can be a cathartic way to honour their memory. Consider turning their paw print into a piece of art.

- **Getting a Tattoo**: A tattoo to honour your pet has become a popular and meaningful tribute. I've seen many beautiful designs—some featuring their pet's face nestled within a paw print, others as simple yet powerful line drawings. A friend once shared, *"Since I got my tattoo, I feel complete. I know my girl is with me all the time. Whenever I feel wobbly, I look down and know she's there to support me."*

- **Helping Others**: Turning your grief into action can be incredibly healing. By helping others and their pets, you honour your pet's memory and find a renewed sense of purpose.

Ways to Honour Your Pet:

- **Pet Sit:** Offer to sit for a friend or neighbour and spend some quality time with their pet.

- **Donate:** Contribute to a cause that supports animals, whether through monetary donations or supplies like food and toys.

- **Foster:** If you feel ready, consider fostering a pet in need. This temporary commitment can bring companionship while making a difference in a pet's life.

- **Fundraiser:** Attend a fundraiser to help animals in rescue, it might be a Trivia night, or a walk to raise funds. There are so many fundraising events, and the best part is that you are helping raise funds for a charity, and you'll also get to meet a tribe of dedicated animal lovers just like yourself.

Sharing Stories and Celebrating Their Life

Sharing stories about your pet can be a healing way to keep their memory alive. By celebrating their life and impact on you, you ensure their spirit continues to bring joy.

- **Writing About Your Pet**: Consider writing down your favourite memories, funny moments, or lessons your pet taught you. This could be a journal, a blog, or even a book.

- **Telling Their Story**: Share stories about your pet with friends, family, or in online communities. Many people find comfort in connecting with others who understand their bond with their pet.

- **Pet Tribute Videos**: Create a video slideshow with photos and videos of your pet set to music. What a beautiful way to reflect on your time together and share their story with others.

- **Celebration of Life**: Host a small gathering of close friends and family to celebrate your pet's life. Share memories, light candles, and perhaps even plant a tree or release biodegradable balloons in their honour.

Keeping Their Spirit Alive Through Rituals

Rituals can provide a sense of continuity and connection to your pet's spirit. They help you create moments of reflection and honour your ongoing bond.

- **Daily or Weekly Rituals**: Set aside time to light a candle, talk to your pet, or meditate while holding their photo or a keepsake. These small acts can bring comfort and a sense of closeness.

- **Special Dates**: Honour your pet on significant dates, such as their birthday or the anniversary of their passing. You might bake their favourite treat or spend the day doing something they loved, like walking in their favourite park.

- **Connecting Th ough Nature**: Many people feel closest to their pets when they spend time in nature. Take walks in places your pet loved, or sit outside and reflect on your bond.

- **Creative Rituals**: Engage in creative activities that remind you of your pet, such as painting, writing poetry, or crafting. These acts can help channel your emotions into something meaningful.

One of my favourite pages to follow on Facebook is **"Team Golden Oldies."** Many years ago, when volunteering at a Golden Retriever rescue, I met Lisa, an incredible woman with a heart of gold. She set out on a mission to adopt senior Golden Retrievers, giving them the love and care they deserve in their golden years.

Over time, her small group of *old souls* has grown, and while the *packages of dogs* she welcomes may have changed, her message and purpose remain the same—every senior dog deserves a loving home.

If you get a chance, I highly recommend visiting Lisa's page. She shares heartwarming stories of her senior rescues and creates beautiful suncatchers (www.fb.com/loveandlightinheart) to raise funds directly toward caring for these special dogs. Every purchase helps support her mission, making a real difference in the lives of these beautiful old souls.

Team Golden Oldies

www.fb.com/TeamGoldenOldies

Hi friends, Lisa here.

I want to talk about a subject that, sadly, I have had to deal with a lot - Grief. I understand and fully appreciate that the way people deal with grief is as individual as the number of people reading this. No two ways are the same, and there is no correct way. I can only speak from my perspective, from my journey with adopting seniors and having the Oldies in my life, and then having to say goodbye.

Since starting TGO nearly 11 years ago, I have lost 31 dogs, not to mention Ian. I've lost three dogs in the past 14 weeks. People often say to me I don't know how you do it. I'll be honest, it's NOT easy. Every time I lose a dog, they take a piece of my heart with them. It is like a door closes to a room they occupied in my heart. But I always ask a dog we lose to send us another. And they do ... I don't do this to 'replace them' and I hope people don't feel that is my intention. But sadly, there are so many senior dogs out there looking for a forever home.

When a new dog arrives, another door to another room seems to open in my heart. A door I didn't even know existed. The heart is amazing like that. It has the capacity and the capability to keep loving and giving. Sometimes I feel my heart is like a revolving door, opening, closing, opening, closing. So often I hear from people that they couldn't possibly get another dog because the pain was too much, losing them.

Although I respect their choice, I do feel sad for them. Sadly, they are denying themselves the opportunity to love again. It is unfortunate for the dog sitting in a pound or shelter, waiting and hoping for love and a forever home to see out their days. The sad truth is that losing something or someone we love hurts. There is no denying that. *But FOR ME I have always felt that it is better to have known a dog, to have loved a dog, for a few years, or even a few months, than to have never known them at all.*

I am under no illusions that the seniors I adopt will be in my life for a long time. I knew from the start that our journey together would be short. Although some might find this confronting or even depressing, I consider it a positive. I try to make EVERY day count, make every day one of love. I provide as many opportunities as possible for the oldies to give and receive as much love as possible in whatever time they have with me. I do not take our time together for granted, for the truth is, each day I spend with the oldies is a gift.

Having the privilege of giving an old dog a safe and loving home to rest their weary head is truly a blessing. I so wish more people could understand this. It is a gift I can give them, perhaps the ultimate gift.

In many ways, I have to shut down my grief, my feelings. Whether this is healthy, I don't know. But the truth is, I have 11 other dogs who need me. I cannot get 'bogged down' in the sadness and loss. It does NOT mean that their death has not affected me, how could it not?. But I guess I push down many of my feelings to continue to do what I do.

That is, to continue to adopt senior dogs. If I didn't, there is no way that I could continually open up my home, but more importantly, my heart for the inevitable loss that is 'just around the corner'.

I try very hard not to get lost in the sadness when I lose an oldie … I am NOT saying this is easy. In fact, it is VERY challenging sometimes!! But I try to remember and to celebrate the time we DID spend together. To rejoice that our paths crossed, that they chose me and I chose them for however long. This approach does NOT make the pain go away. But I guess it makes it bearable. The truth is, each dog who has come into my life has taught me something. For that, I will be forever grateful.

My message to all who read this is to embrace each and every day you have with your furkid. To not take any day for granted. Because the truth is, you never know when it will be your last. This message also applies to others in your life who you love and care for. Tell them and show them EVERY day how much you love them because one day, sometimes when you least expect it, they won't be there to tell ….
Lisa xx

> *'Saving one dog will not change the world, but surely for that one dog, the world will change forever.'*

10 Ways to Honour Your Pet's Memory

1. **Adopt or Foster in Their Honou** : If and when you're ready, consider adopting or fostering another animal in need. This can be a beautiful way to honour your pet's legacy.

2. **Volunteer for Animal Causes**: Donate your time or resources to a local animal shelter, rescue group, or wildlife organisation in your pet's name.

3. **Create a Pet Memorial Website**: Build a digital space to share photos, stories, and memories of your pet. This can also serve as a way for friends and family to contribute their memories.

4. **Donate to Animal Charities**: Donate in your pet's name to an organisation that aligns with their spirit, such as a shelter, conservation group, or therapy animal program.

5. **Plant a Tree Through a Charity**: Many organisations offer programs where you can plant a tree in your pet's name, providing a living legacy while supporting the environment.

6. **Frame Their Paw Print**: If you have a paw print mould or impression, frame it with their photo to create a special keepsake.

7. **Host a Fundraiser**: Organise an event or fundraiser to support causes your pet would have loved, such as raising funds for medical care for rescue animals.

8. **Create a Tribute Stone**: Design a custom engraved stone or plaque to place in your garden or a special location.

9. **Join or Start a Support Group**: Sharing your grief with others who have experienced similar loss can be profoundly healing. Consider starting a group to honour your pet while helping others.

10. **Carry Their Memory with You**: Whether it's a locket with their photo, a bracelet with their name, or a keychain with a charm, carrying something tangible can bring comfort.

Closing Thought

Honouring your pet's memory is a profoundly personal journey. There is no right or wrong way to remember them—only what feels right to you. Each gesture, big or small, is a testament to the love and bond you shared. By celebrating their life and keeping their spirit alive, you ensure that their legacy continues to bring light and joy, even in their physical absence. Remember, your pet's love is eternal, and their memory will forever be a part of your heart.

Koda's memorial Sun catcher with some of his fur incorporated in it.

You can find more examples of these on her facebook page here: www.fb.com/loveandlightinheart

Chapter 13

Will I Ever Feel Normal Again?

Grieving the loss of a beloved pet can leave a profound emptiness in your heart and disrupt your daily life in ways you never anticipated. Many people I speak with in my sessions share a deep fear: they wonder if moving forward will make it seem like they've forgotten their pet. They struggle with the concept of a "normal" life without their cherished companion by their side. This chapter explores how to define a new normal, accept the evolution of grief, focus on progress rather than perfection, and embrace the healing journey in your own time and way.

Defining a New Normal

After losing a pet, life will never feel the same, and that's okay. Your daily routines may have revolved around your pet, from morning walks to evening cuddles, and now you're faced with the daunting task of navigating life without them. Many pet parents ask, "How do I go on without them?"

It's important to remember that there is no "right" way to grieve or move forward. Some people choose to carry their pet's urn with them in the car or to work as a source of comfort. Others may continue setting out their pet's water bowl for weeks or months after their passing. These rituals are deeply personal and can bridge the life you knew and the new normal you are creating.

The *New Normal* is whatever feels right for you. Whether it's wearing a piece of jewellery, getting a tattoo, or carrying a tiny urn, it's about what brings you comfort. Adjust your routine gradually, taking small steps forward. And if you take a step backward now and then, that's okay—grief has no timeline. Be kind to yourself and allow the time and space you need to adjust to life without your beloved pet.

Accepting the Evolution of Grief

Grief is not something you "get over"—it's something you learn to live with. Over time, the sharp pain of loss may soften into a quieter ache, but it will always be a part of you because your love for your pet is a part of you. Accepting this evolution doesn't mean forgetting your pet; it means finding ways to carry their memory with you while allowing yourself to heal.

In my animal communication sessions, I've often heard pet parents worry that if they start to feel happy again, it might mean they're moving on or leaving their pet behind. This couldn't be further from the truth. Your pet loved you unconditionally, and they wouldn't want you to live in perpetual sadness. Moving forward is not a betrayal of their memory—it's a testament to the love and joy they brought into your life.

How Grief Changes Over Time:

- **Early Grief:** This stage often feels overwhelming, with emotions like sadness, anger, guilt, and disbelief crashing over you like waves.

- **Adjustment Period:** As time passes, you may find moments of normalcy, though triggers like a favourite toy or a special date can bring grief back to the surface.
- **Integration:** Eventually, your grief becomes a part of who you are, but it doesn't dominate your life. You carry your pet's memory with you in a natural and comforting way.

Focusing on Progress, Not Perfection

One of the most important things to remember during your healing journey is that progress isn't linear. There will be good and bad days, and that's completely normal. Healing doesn't mean you'll never feel sad again—it means you'll start to find joy alongside the sadness.

Many pet parents feel pressure to "move on" or "get over it" quickly, especially if they sense that others don't understand their grief. But grief isn't something you can rush. Focus on small steps forward, rather than forcing yourself to feel a certain way.

Signs of Progress to Celebrate:

- Smiling when you think about a happy memory with your pet.
- Reconnecting with activities or hobbies you enjoyed before your loss.
- Feeling less guilty about taking care of yourself and finding joy again.

Letting Go of Perfection: It's okay to have setbacks. You might feel like you're doing fine one day and then be overwhelmed with sadness the next. This doesn't mean you're failing—it means you're human. Be gentle with yourself and recognise that healing is a journey, not a destination.

Embracing the Healing Journey

The healing journey is unique for everyone. Some people find comfort in creating a memorial for their pet, while others focus on new routines or even bringing a new pet into their life when they feel ready. Whatever path you choose, the goal is to find a balance between honouring your pet's memory and embracing the life ahead of you.

Journal Prompts for Moving Forward:

1. What is your new normal, and how can you make it meaningful?
2. Write about a moment when you felt your pet's presence after their passing.
3. How can you honour your pet's memory in your daily life?
4. Reflect on how your grief has evolved since your pet's passing. What has changed?
5. Write a letter to your pet about what you miss most and how you're trying to move forward.
6. List three small steps you can take to find joy again.
7. What did your pet teach you about resilience and love, and how can you carry those lessons forward?
8. Write about a time you felt happy since your pet's passing. How did it feel, and what contributed to that happiness?
9. Describe what you imagine your pet would say to you if they could reassure you from the afterlife.
10. What are you grateful for in your relationship with your pet, and how can you express that gratitude?

Moving Forward Without Leaving Them Behind

Moving forward without your pet can feel daunting, but it's important to remember that moving forward doesn't mean leaving them behind. Your pet's memory will always be a part of you, woven into the fabric of who you are. They have shaped your heart and your life in ways that will remain forever.

As you navigate your new normal, focus on carrying their love with you. Talk to them, think of them, and honour them in whatever way feels right. Whether through a daily ritual, a tribute, or simply holding them in your thoughts, your bond with your pet is eternal.

Final Thought

Grief is a journey, not a destination. There's no magic moment when everything suddenly feels okay, but you'll find a new rhythm to life over time. Be patient with yourself, celebrate the small victories, and trust that your pet's love will guide you through. While life may never feel "normal" as it once did, you will create a new normal filled with the love, memories, and lessons your pet gave you. And that, in its way, is a beautiful tribute to the bond you shared.

Chapter 14

Signs Your Pet Is Still With You

Losing a beloved pet leaves a void that can feel impossible to fill. Yet, many pet parents report experiencing signs that their pets are still with them in spirit. These moments can bring profound comfort and reassurance, offering a sense of connection that transcends physical boundaries. This chapter will explore how pets communicate after passing, how to recognise these signs, and how to open yourself to these experiences. We will also share stories from pet parents who have found solace in knowing their pets are still with them.

Understanding Signs from the Afterlife

When a pet dies, their physical presence may be gone, but their energy and love remain. Many people take comfort in the belief that their pets, like humans, send signs from the afterlife. These signs are often subtle, requiring us to pay attention and trust our intuition.

Pet parents often describe feelings of their pet's presence, noticing unusual occurrences, or receiving direct signs that seem to carry personal meaning. Each individual uniquely experiences and interprets these signs differently, yet they all share a profound sense of connection.

Common Ways Pets Communicate After Passing

Pets have a variety of ways to let us know they are still with us. Here are some of the most commonly reported signs:

1. **Dreams:** Many pet parents report vivid dreams where their pet appears happy, healthy, and peaceful. These dreams often feel more real and impactful than ordinary dreams, leaving a lasting impression.
2. **Sounds:** You might hear familiar noises, such as the sound of your pet's paws on the floor, their bark or meow, or even the jingling of their collar.
3. **Smells:** Some people notice the scent of their pet's fur or favourite treats, even when there's no physical source for the smell.
4. **Physical Sensations:** Feeling your pet's presence, such as the weight of their body on the bed or a gentle nudge, is a common experience.
5. **Signs in Nature:** Animals often use nature as a medium to send messages. Butterflies, birds, or other animals behaving unusually around you may carry your pet's energy.
6. **Coincidences and Synchronicities:** Repeatedly encountering your pet's name, numbers associated with them (such as their adoption date), or other meaningful coincidences can be their way of reaching out.
7. **Objects Moving or Appearing:** Some pet parents notice their pet's toys, beds, or other belongings moving or appearing in unexpected places.
8. **Feeling Their Energy:** This might be a general sense of warmth, love, or comfort, as though your pet is watching over you.

How to Open Yourself to These Connections

While these signs often occur spontaneously, there are ways to create an environment that encourages connection with your pet's spirit. Here are some practices to help you:

1. **Be Open and Receptive:** Trust that your pet's love for you continues beyond their physical presence. Let go of doubt and allow yourself to believe in the possibility of connection.

2. **Meditate:** Quiet your mind through meditation. Visualise your pet in a happy and peaceful place, and invite them to share their presence with you. Pay attention to any sensations, images, or feelings that arise.

3. **Set an Intention:** Before going to sleep or starting your day, set an intention to receive a sign from your pet. Be specific about what you're looking for, but also stay open to other forms of communication.

4. **Keep a Journal:** Record any signs or feelings you experience. Writing down these moments helps you recognise patterns and validate your experiences over time.

5. **Create a Sacred Space:** Dedicate a space in your home to your pet's memory. Display their photos, keepsakes, or a candle. This space can serve as a focal point for your connection.

6. **Talk to Them** Speak to your pet as if they were still with you. Share your thoughts, feelings, and love. Often, you'll find comfort in the act of communication itself.

7. **Seek Guidance:** If you struggle to connect with your pet's spirit, consider working with an animal communicator or intuitive who specialises in pets in spirit, such as myself.

Feel free to reach out via my website

www.donnadolittle.com.au

Stories of Comfort from Other Pet Parents

Hearing about others' experiences can be incredibly validating and comforting. Here are some stories from pet parents who have felt their pets' presence after passing:

Anna and Max: Anna lost her Labrador, Max, after 12 wonderful years together. A week after his passing, Anna was sitting in her garden when she noticed a butterfly land on her hand. The butterfly stayed with her for several minutes, and Anna felt an overwhelming sense of peace. She later realised that Max used to chase butterflies in the garden, believing this was his way of saying he was still with her.

David and Bella: David's cat, Bella, passed away unexpectedly. In the days following her passing, David began hearing soft meows at night. At first, he dismissed it as his imagination, but the sounds continued. One evening, he felt a warm, comforting presence on his bed—as if Bella had curled up next to him, just like she always did.

Sophie and Toby: Sophie's Border Collie, Toby, had been her constant companion for 10 years. After his passing, Sophie noticed that Toby's favourite toy, a squeaky duck, would appear in different spots around the house. Even though she hadn't touched it, the toy seemed to move on its own. Sophie took this as a sign that Toby was still watching over her.

Chloe: The day after her passing, I found myself searching Facebook, and somehow I had ended up on an ad in the marketplace for dog bowls. Right before my eyes, there was a dog bowl with the name "Miss Chloe" on it. I loved calling her that name.

Ajax: He is always around, leaving me constant messages and signs. Just a few weeks ago, while on holiday in a small town in NSW called *Scone*—a place deeply connected to horses—I had a moment that made me laugh out loud. The town has plaques on the footpaths honouring famous horses, from stock horses to racehorses and polo champions. As I walked along, at that exact moment, something caught my eye. I looked down, and right between my feet was a plaque that read **"Ajax."** I couldn't stop laughing.

On the first anniversary of Ajax's passing, another sign came in the most unexpected way. A dog-themed plaque reading *"All you need is love… and a dog"* suddenly fell from the ledge and landed on his bed. Later that same day, I walked into the room where he had passed, and his familiar scent overwhelmed me. I felt drawn to a plastic container sitting in plain sight for ages. When I opened it, I found it was full of his hair. I had no memory of ever placing it there, and I had no idea why it was even in that container, but in that moment, I *knew* it was him.

I could fill an entire book with stories of messages and signs from pets in spirit. The most important thing I want to share is this: **be open to receiving them.** So often, people tell me, *Oh, I saw this, and it reminded me of my precious dog or cat, but I thought I was imagining it.* But think—if your pet worked so hard to send you a sign, how heartbreaking it must be for them when you dismiss it.

Write down what you see, hear, and feel in a journal. Over time, you'll begin to notice the patterns, the little *winks* from your beloved pet, reminding you that they are still with you. Even though they are in spirit, their love never leaves.

Finding Comfort in Their Presence

Recognising signs from your pet and believing in their ongoing presence can help ease the pain of their loss. These moments remind us that our bond with our pets is eternal, and their love continues to surround us. Whether through dreams, nature, or an unexpected sign, these experiences offer reassurance that our pets remain a part of our lives, even after crossing the Rainbow Bridge.

Moving Forward Together

While it may take time to fully embrace the signs your pet is sending, know their love for you is unchanging. As you navigate your grief, allow these connections to comfort you and remind you of the special bond you shared. You are not alone on this journey, and your pet's spirit is always near, guiding and loving you every step of the way.

"We were meant to find each other — and we always will, again and again."

Chapter 15

Rituals and Ceremonies for Closure

*S*aying goodbye to a beloved pet is one of our most profound moments as animal guardians. Rituals provide comfort, structure, and a sense of closure, helping us process our grief while honouring the love we shared. A carefully created ceremony—whether simple or elaborate—can provide space for reflection, remembrance, and healing.

Why Rituals Are Important for Healing

Grief is a profoundly personal journey, and rituals serve as gentle touchstones that help guide us through the emotions of loss. They provide an opportunity to express love, gratitude, and sorrow tangibly. Rituals can also be a way to involve family and friends, allowing them to share in both the loss and the cherished memories of a pet's life.

Rituals do not have to be grand or complicated to be meaningful. Even the simplest gestures can be deeply healing when done with intention. Here are five simple yet powerful rituals to honour a pet's passing:

Five Simple Rituals to Honour a Pet's Memory

1. Lighting a Candle

A candle symbolises light, love, and the eternal connection between you and your pet. Choose a quiet time to light a candle in their honour. As the flame flickers, please take a moment to reflect on the joy and companionship they brought into your life. You can say a few words, such as:

> *"May this flame symbolise the love that will always burn in my heart for you."*

You may light a candle on special occasions—birthdays, anniversaries, or even a moment when you need to connect.

2. Writing a Letter to Your Pet

Writing can be a cathartic way to express emotions that may be difficult to speak aloud. Consider writing a letter to your pet, sharing everything you want them to know. This could include:

- A thank-you for the love they gave
- Special memories you cherish
- How much they meant to you

After writing, you may keep the letter in a special place, place it in a memorial box, or even read it aloud during a ceremony.

3. Creating a Memory Stone

A memory stone is a simple yet meaningful way to honour a pet. Find a smooth stone and paint or engrave it with your pet's name, a paw print, or a special word that reminds you of them. This stone can be placed in the garden, by their favourite resting spot, or somewhere in your home where you'll see it often.

Some people create a small stack of stones, adding one each time they want to send a thought or message to their pet in spirit.

4. Setting Up a Dedicated Space

Creating a small tribute area in your home or garden helps keep your pet's memory close. I even know a person who set up a space in their car on the dashboard, as this is where they spent the most amount of time. This could include:

- A framed photo
- Their collar or favourite toy
- A candle or small figurine

This space is a comforting place to reflect and feel their presence whenever needed.

5. The Farewell Walk

Taking a final walk in a place your pet loved can be a moving way to say goodbye. As you walk, reflect on the moments you shared in that place. If you feel called, you can speak to them, tell them stories, or walk in silence, feeling their presence beside you.

Some people choose to leave a small token—a flower, a note, or a special object—as a symbol of remembrance.

How to Create a Personalised Ceremony

A personalised ceremony allows you to honour your pet's life in a way that feels most meaningful to you. There is no right or wrong way to do this—follow what feels true to your heart. Below is a suggested structure for a heartfelt ceremony that can be adapted to fit your needs.

A Ceremony for Friends and Family

This ceremony is ideal for those who wish to gather family and friends in a shared space to celebrate their pet's life.

Preparation:

- Choose a meaningful location (eg, the garden, a park, or a favourite spot your pet loved).
- Invite those who loved your pet to attend.
- Ask guests to bring something that reminds them of your pet—a photo, a written memory, a flower, or an item from nature.

The Ceremony Structure:

1. **Opening words** – Begin by welcoming everyone and expressing the purpose of the gathering. You might say:
2. "We are here today to honour and celebrate the life of [pet's name], who brought so much joy and love into our lives."
3. **Sharing stories and memories** – Invite each person to share a short memory, story, or reflection about your pet. A funny moment, a heartwarming story, or simply the meaning they held can capture their essence.
4. **Symbolic gesture** – Each guest can place their token (flower, stone, or note) in a central place, such as a memorial space, under a tree, or by the pet's favourite spot.
5. **Moment of silence** – Take a few quiet moments to reflect, offering love and gratitude for the time you shared.
6. **Closing words** – End the ceremony with a farewell message, a poem, or a simple phrase such as:

"Though [pet's name] is no longer physically here, their spirit lives on in our hearts. May their love continue to guide us."

After the ceremony, people may choose to stay and talk, share a meal, or sit in quiet reflection.

Story of a Little Blue Heeler

We lived on a dual-living property next door to my mum and sister, so Kayla, the blue heeler, was loved by everyone. She had a habit of wandering from house to house, always following the scent of a BBQ or the sound of people gathered—wherever the action was, that's where you'd find her. She truly loved being around people.

When she passed away, we buried her in the front garden of the house that had been her home for the last ten years. But knowing it wasn't our forever home, we decided to buy a statue to place there in her memory. We held a small ceremony to say goodbye; the statue meant that when we eventually moved, a part of her could come with us.

During the ceremony, each family member shared a memory of Kayla. There were tears and plenty of laughter as we remembered the cheeky, loving dog she was. We also shared this poem.

With a coat like the sky and a spirit so bright,
A little blue heeler brought joy and delight.
Her stumpy tail wiggled, so short and so round,
Like a wombat, she wobbled, so close to the ground.
She loved a good BBQ, nose in the air,
Like a wombat, she wobbled, so close to the ground.
She loved a good BBQ, nose in the air,
Hoping for scraps with a hopeful stare.
A sausage, a steak—she'd never say no,
Her belly was happy when the grill was aglow.
But when storms rolled in with a thunderous roar,
She'd tremble and hide, paws pressed to the floor.

> No bark, no bravado, just wide, worried eyes,
> Seeking a lap where she'd quietly lie.
> Yet when her dad dove into the deep,
> She'd race to the shore in a bounding leap.
> A rescue dog's heart, so loyal and true,
> She'd paddle and bark till he came into view.
> Through sunshine and rain, through laughter and tears,
> She gave us her love for so many years.
> A little blue heeler, small but so grand,
> With a heart full of love and a paw in our hand.

Holding Space in Those Final Moments

When the time comes to say goodbye, creating a sacred and loving space can bring comfort and deep connection for both you and your beloved pet. Holding space means being fully present: emotionally, spiritually, and energetically. It's about softening into the moment, allowing it to unfold with tenderness, and honouring your pet's journey with grace.

A vet once suggested giving your pet all the things they were never allowed, yes, even chocolate, because every soul deserves a final taste of joy.

One friend shared how their family created a circle of fresh flowers and fairy lights in a peaceful bushland corner where their dog loved to rest. It became the sacred space for his final goodbye—surrounded by love and the energy of home. These moments, held in love and ceremony, become sacred threads woven into your pet's final journey, offering comfort, beauty, and peace.

Incorporating Spiritual Practices (If Desired)

For those who find comfort in spiritual practices, consider adding elements that align with your beliefs. This could include:

- **Burning sage or incense** – A cleansing ritual to create a peaceful space.
- **Reading a poem or prayer** – Words that resonate with love and remembrance.
- **Playing soft music or nature sounds** – Creates a soothing atmosphere to reflect and heal.

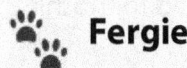 **Fergie**

We crossed paths when I offered to foster you through the Golden Retriever Rescue. You were 9 1/2 years old—a senior dog. The rescue shelter told me seniors can be hard to rehome due to their age and medical issues. I saw you were shut down the moment you walked into my house. You feared so many things: the lead, plastic bags, loud noises, and water!

We were a busy household, full of love, and it broke my heart to watch you. You didn't know how to play, you didn't want to engage with the other dogs, and while you loved going for walks, you completely shut down if we went near water. Every Sunday, as a family, we walked on the beach, swam, and played near the river—something we had done for six years.

The day you did a zoomie around the house, jumped up on the lounge, and acted like a puppy, I cried tears of love and joy. You were finally living the life you deserved.

You were the reason I became an animal communicator. The lady who delivered you to us from the rescue offered me an animal communication session. I had no idea what that was, or that people could even intuitively connect with animals. The communicator was in Peru, I was in Australia—and there I was, with you and all the other animals in our household, gathered around the computer, listening. The call woke something deep within me, and I knew this was my soul journey, what I was meant to do with my life, and how I could help people and their pets.

You brought me so much joy. You were a total love bug. I could lie and cuddle you for hours—you asked for nothing, yet you gave everything.

At 16 years old, I decided we needed a party, because how many Golden Retrievers make it to that age! You sat on your soft bed and proudly wore a party hat. Family members and lots of doggies surrounded you. Of course, you tried to eat all of the doggie cake ... we laughed and took lots of pictures. Everyone's hearts were full.

A month and one day later, I knew it was your time to say goodbye. I didn't want to let you go, but I knew you were tired—your body didn't have the strength to get up anymore. We spent the day outside on the grass, cuddling, talking, and eating treats. Lil Jess and Ajax sat with us—I felt like we were all laughing and crying and just being in this beautiful love bubble.

I brought you inside and began to prepare for when the vet arrived. I made you a comfortable bed. I brushed you—oh, your coat looked magnificent. You smelled divine and radiated love from those beautiful eyes of yours.

> I played music and did a meditation while sitting with you, sharing my thoughts and the love we shared. Tears rolled down my face; my shirt was soaked, but I didn't care in that moment. In my meditation, you transformed from this beautiful cream Golden Retriever—so proud—into a massive, majestic white wolf who stood beside me to protect me. You shared a message that I will always hold in my heart.
>
> I know, one day... we will meet at the Rainbow Bridge, and you'll show me around. Always the gentleman, always the one to make sure everyone else is okay.
>
> I love you, my big love bug. Thank you for coming into my life and sharing your love and wisdom.
>
> Donna

Closing Thought

Rituals and ceremonies are deeply personal, and there is no "right" way to say goodbye. Whether by lighting a candle, writing a letter, or gathering loved ones for a shared ceremony, these acts of love and remembrance help us process grief while celebrating the unbroken bond.

Your pet's love was unique, and so should be how you honour them. Take your time, trust your heart, and create a farewell that reflects the depth of the love you shared.

Chapter 16

When To Consider A New Pet

The question of whether to bring a new pet into your home is very common in my animal communication sessions. It's a deeply personal decision, layered with emotions, memories, and sometimes even guilt. For many, the thought of sharing their heart again feels impossible. For others, it feels like the natural next step. Whatever your journey, this chapter will guide you in understanding when you might be ready, navigating the complex emotions that come with this decision, and honouring your past pet while opening your heart to another.

Knowing When You're Ready

Deciding to bring a new pet into your life isn't about replacing the one that passed —it's about recognising when your heart is ready to share love again. For some, this happens quickly; for others, it takes months or even years. And that's okay.

As an animal communicator, I receive messages from pets in spirit, lovingly encouraging their guardians to consider bringing another animal into their lives. The timing, however, is unique to each person. Here are a few signs that you might be ready:

1. **You feel it's time:** The ache of grief begins to soften, making space for the idea of bringing a new family member home.

2. **You miss the companionship:** Your home feels empty, or your daily routines feel incomplete without the presence of a pet.

3. **Your life is incomplete:** Without a pet, you feel like something is missing in your life. They were your companion and best friend, and without them, life isn't the same.

4. **You find joy in memories:** Instead of feeling only pain, you smile when you think of your past pet and the joy they brought into your life.

5. **You find yourself looking at rescue sites:** You keep telling yourself you are just looking, but the pull to go and look has become strong, and you wonder if it's the right time.

Letting Go of Guilt for Moving Forward

One of the most common barriers to welcoming a new pet is guilt. Many pet parents feel they're betraying their beloved companion by even considering bringing another animal into their lives.

In my sessions, I often use a deck of Oracle Cards called *Animal Messages and Signs from the Rainbow Bridge* to help facilitate communication with pets in spirit. When shuffling the cards, sometimes one will fall or jump out of the deck on its own. One particular card tends to evoke a strong emotional reaction: **"Sending You a New Pet."**

When this card appears, I often witness a mix of emotions—relief, joy, hesitation, or even resistance.

One client, for example, broke into tears of relief when this card appeared. They had already brought a new pet into their home, but feared their previous pet might feel replaced or hurt. The card brought them comfort, reminding them that their love for their new pet was not a betrayal but a continuation of the love they had always carried.

Others, however, react with hesitation: *"Oh no, I could never do that. What if "Gus' feels like I'm replacing him?"* The truth is, your pet in spirit will never feel replaced. They know the depth of your love and want nothing more than for you to share it with another animal who needs it.

Honouring Your Past Pet While Loving Another

Welcoming a new pet doesn't mean leaving your past pet behind—it's about carrying their memory with you while opening your heart to a new chapter. The love and lessons from your past pet can live on in the way you care for your new companion.

While you might choose to keep a special toy as a cherished keepsake, sharing the toy pile can bring unexpected joy. Ajax never played with half of the toys he had collected, yet when Snowy arrived, every single toy in the basket was dragged out, played with, or completely destroyed. One toy, a Christmas candy cane, had been sitting untouched for two years. I had even considered throwing it away. Every time I see Snowy playing with it, I smile, knowing Ajax would be happy to share his toys with our new dog.

Not a day goes by that I don't think about or talk about one of my past pets. With so many beloved companions over the years, their stories naturally weave into my daily life. Sharing memories of your pets in spirit celebrates their presence and deepens your everlasting connection.

Rosie & Hank

I was doing my best to be an adult and work through the horrendous grief of unexpectedly losing both my Greyhounds, Rosie and Hank, within just five weeks of each other. It was heartbreaking, and I felt utterly shattered.

Then along came Ellie—a rescue Greyhound who desperately needed a home. I took her in, hoping that maybe we could heal together. But after three months, I couldn't shake the feeling that Ellie wasn't happy. She was incredibly clingy and always seemed worried, like she was walking on eggshells. I didn't know how to help her, and I even wondered if she'd be better off with someone else.

So, I did what we all do—I turned to Google. I typed in the usual frantic questions: *"Does my dog like me?" "Why doesn't my dog like me?" "How do I know if my dog is sad?"*

That's when I came across Donna's website - www.donnadolittle.com.au

I didn't know much about Animal Communication then, but something nudged me to book a session. And I'm so glad I did—because I was speechless from the very first moment.

With just a photo and Ellie's age, Donna connected with her and told me precisely what Ellie had been feeling. She explained that Ellie *wanted* to be with me—she wasn't sure if this was her forever home. She was uncertain and a little lost.

But that wasn't all.

Through Ellie, Donna shared a story, one that had deeply affected Ellie's sense of safety and trust. It was linked to a past situation involving someone I once considered a friend. The details Donna described were so specific, so accurate, it was as if someone had phoned her beforehand and told her everything. But no one had. Ellie had.

That moment changed everything for me. I'd always felt that Ellie came to me not just to be rescued, but to rescue *me*. Donna confirmed it. And in doing so, she helped shift our entire relationship.

Donna is truly one of the most caring, compassionate humans I've ever met—even if it's only been over Zoom! We've since had another session for my Greyhound boy Simon, who suddenly developed a fear of birds (which is probably my fault—I have a bit of a bird phobia myself, and it turns out he picked up on that. Sorry, Simon!)

Donna's dedication to her gift is incredible. She doesn't just communicate with animals—she bridges the emotional gap between them and us. The love she brings into each session, the reassurance she offers, and the confidence she helps build in us as pet parents is nothing short of amazing.

She's taught me not to dismiss my feelings or instincts. She's helped me understand that, yes, our dogs *are* talking to us. We just have to listen more closely.

I can't recommend Donna enough. Honestly, the world needs more Donnas.

> *"Sometimes the ones we rescue are the very souls sent to rescue us."*

Helping a New Pet Find Their Place in Your Heart

Every pet is unique, with their own quirks, personality, and needs. Adjusting to a new companion can be both joyful and challenging. Here are some tips to help you bond with your new pet while embracing your healing journey:

- **Take It Slow:** Allow time for both you and your new pet to adjust. Building a bond takes patience and care.

- **Acknowledge Your Emotions:** It's okay to feel a mix of emotions—happiness, guilt, sadness, or even fear. Recognise these feelings as part of the healing process.

- **Find Joy in the Differences** Celebrate how your new pet differs from your past companion. These differences are what make them special.

Be gentle with yourself. A new pet will also try to find their way into your life. They won't know how you do things in your family. If it's a puppy, they may have accidents, chew things and climb all over the lounge. Remember, they are learning the ropes (just as your old pet did when they arrived).

If you've taken on a rescue pet, they can come with their own challenges. After Ajax passed, my local rescue asked if I could foster a dog. I wasn't ready for another pet, and it took me a few days to say yes. It was only supposed to be for a few weeks—they assured me he'd be adopted quickly since he was a small dog. But I wasn't sure if I was up to the challenge, and I worried about how my little old dog, Lil Jess, at 19 years old, would cope with an energetic foster.

I don't know what possessed me to agree, but soon I found myself driving to the rescue with Lil Jess in tow to meet a "Mini Fox Terrier." I reassured myself that it would be okay—Mini Foxies typically weigh around 4–5 kg, not much bigger than Jess. Having owned a Mini Foxie and a Tenterfield Terrier before, I figured I understood the breed.

Then a rescue worker walked out with the dog. I looked up and immediately said, "You know that's not a Mini Fox Terrier?" He was at least 10 kg strong, lean, and built like an athlete. I wanted to cry. What had I done? Before I could object, they bundled him into my car, handed me leads, food, and an old bed, and said goodbye. Not before telling me, "He has separation anxiety, can be aggressive with other dogs, is an escape artist, doesn't walk well on a lead, and just didn't fit into his previous family."

Welcome to Snowy

He had been purchased during lockdown and had very little training, and now here I was, bringing him home to my frail, elderly dog. I wanted to cry—and if I'm honest, I did. All the way home.

"Your pets in spirit know exactly what you need."

When we arrived home, Snowy tore apart the toys, ran in circles chasing his tail, and barked nonstop as he zoomed up and down the outside deck. Living on a canal, I panicked that he'd fall in and become shark food. When he finally came inside, I tried feeding him, hoping it would calm him. For three days he ignored all food given to him. He had been fed on Pal dog food and disliked the premium food offered. He turned up his nose and wasn't having a bit of it. He shook constantly, clearly distressed, and dealt with his anxiety by destroying anything he could get his mouth on—rocks, plants, toys.

The next morning, I decided to walk him. *What could go wrong?* I thought it would help burn off some of his boundless energy. He seemed calmer, and since he appeared confident, I figured a long walk would be good for both of us. But the moment we saw another dog, he transformed. He lunged, growled, and barked like a dog possessed. Fortunately, most people in my neighbourhood know me, so they ignored my sudden appearance with a reactive dog.

I left him in the backyard with a toy when we got home. Thirty minutes later, I checked on him—he was gone. Then I saw him. He had climbed under the side fence and was sitting on the neighbour's outdoor table, grinning as if to say, *Look at me! I can do whatever I want!* Within 24 hours, he had displayed every challenging behaviour the rescue had warned about.

I called the rescue and said, "I can't do this." I had owned plenty of dogs, but none were ever reactive or had this level of high energy. After a lot of persuasion, they offered training and convinced me to try for another week. They assured me he'd be adopted quickly.

There was even talk of medicating him. But I wasn't sure that was the answer. This boy needed love, patience, and a kind soul to help him become the dog he was meant to be. A friend dropped off a different lead, and the following morning, I tried again to walk him, hoping our morning walk would be a lot more eventful than the previous day. As a foster guardian, you want to help the dog become the best version of themselves in preparation for their new family.

I took Snowy to four meet-and-greets. I wasn't optimistic about how he'd react to other dogs each time. He was beautiful but misunderstood—he needed structure, training, and love. Every meet-and-greet, I cried all the way there and back. Was I crying for him, because he had been abandoned? Or was I crying as I was grieving Ajax? And then there was the anticipatory grief—Lil Jess was nearing the end of her life, and I felt guilty that Snowy demanded so much of my time.

Two months after Snowy arrived, Lil Jess passed. I was still mourning Ajax, and now my heart shattered again. Snowy had been with me for three months, and the rescue pressured me to keep him. My partner wasn't supportive—he didn't want another dog and wanted Snowy gone as soon as possible.

One morning, as I walked Snowy, I realised something—he was exactly what I needed to help me through my grief. I laughed at the irony. He was nothing like the dog I thought I wanted. I had begged the universe to give me back Ajax—a big, soft, cuddly, loveable, obedient Golden Retriever. Instead, I got Snowy—a high-energy, stubborn, reactive little terrier.

Snowy got me out walking every day. We trained, played, and healed together. He made me laugh *every single day* at his crazy antics. I had been struggling with anxiety attacks, my heart racing out of nowhere. But instead of focusing on what I thought I wanted, I started focusing on what we both needed.

Snowy is hilarious—I know I keep saying it, but it's true. He acts tough and confident, but he's a total marshmallow. He even made a Cocker Spaniel friend who helped him overcome his fear of other dogs. He wasn't aggressive—just fearful, lacking confidence, and expressing it the only way he knew how.

Snowy has taught me so much—I could probably write half a book about him. We compete in Scent Work, a sport where dogs detect specific odours, something I started with Ajax before he passed. Snowy also does Mantrailing, where he tracks human scents through bushland or urban areas. While we don't compete in Mantrailing, we do in Scent Work—and he has even earned a few pretty ribbons! He thrives on these activities, and together, we've found happiness through them.

He still struggles with separation anxiety, and while we're working with a behaviourist trainer, I often ask myself—what is he reflecting in me? Why is this surfacing for him? It's easy to say he came with that trait, but deep down, I know it mirrors my feelings. Soul contracts are a conversation for another time, but it's a topic I love to explore—how pets mirror and support their guardians on their soul journey.

While Snowy was initially overwhelming, he rewards me and others with so much love. I needed him as much as he needed me. I never would have chosen a dog like him, and I'm certain Ajax knew that. So, he sent Snowy to keep me busy and to show me that I *could* help a dog with challenges using love and my unique abilities.

My journey with Snowy has been a journey through grief. I can't imagine life without a dog, and this time, I clearly needed a challenge.

I hear so many incredible stories of people adopting rescue dogs and the love they share with their new guardians. It's truly special.

"Your pet in spirit will send you the pet you need, not the one you think you want!"

A Story of Love Continuing

I'll never forget a session with a gentleman whose beloved German Shepherd, Mia, had passed suddenly. Mia had been what he described as 'his soulmate', a companion sent, as he believed, by his late wife to watch over him. Mia's sudden passing left him devastated and lost.

As we connected, I shuffled my Oracle Cards. A card fell from the deck without any prompting: **"Sending You a New Pet."** I didn't share this immediately, waiting instead to relay Mia's messages of love and comfort. But as the session progressed, it became clear that Mia had already orchestrated something remarkable.

Through tears, the man shared that, days before our session, a stray dog had appeared at his door. The dog was nervous but wouldn't leave. Mia's message was clear: *"He can't be alone."* She had sent this new companion to him, knowing he needed love and protection in his life.

Bringing this up in our animal communication session allowed him to talk about his feelings and how he was worried she might feel sad or upset that he had replaced her. To the contrary, she wanted him to have another dog ... she knew precisely what he needed and made it happen!

Four months later, the gentleman contacted me again. He told me the dog would jump the fence and go on walkabouts. He felt the dog didn't want to be fenced in. We both laughed when he told me a new little dog called JoJo had arrived at his workplace and needed a loving home. It felt like Mia had made sure her dad had the comfort of a dog until JoJo arrived.

Navigating the Decision

Deciding when to bring a new pet into your life is deeply personal. It's a decision that comes with a mix of joy, guilt, hope, and fear. But remember this: Your heart has an infinite capacity for love. Bringing a new pet into your life doesn't mean letting go of the past—it means carrying your love forward.

If you're still unsure, trust that your pet in spirit will guide you. Their love for you didn't end when they passed, and they'll continue to support you as you navigate this journey. Whether through signs, dreams, or a card falling from a deck, their message will always be one of love and encouragement.

By opening your heart to a new companion, you honour the legacy of your past pet and give another soul the chance to experience the love you so beautifully shared. It's not about replacing; it's about continuing the story of love, one chapter at a time.

Chapter 17

The Journey Of The Soul Animal

When a beloved pet passes, it can feel like a piece of your heart has been torn away. We feel their absence deeply—the quiet that replaces joyful barking, the empty bed that once radiated warmth, the silence where soft paws used to pad through the house. Grief can be all-consuming, but what if I told you that your pet's journey does not end with their physical passing? What if their soul continues to walk beside you, offering love and support in ways unseen?

Our connection with our pets is not limited to their earthly existence. The love we share with them is far greater than the physical body they once inhabited. In this chapter, we'll explore the journey of the animal soul, the possibility of reincarnation, and how you can continue to connect with your pet beyond the physical world.

Exploring the Concept of Animal Souls

Many spiritual traditions, ancient cultures, and intuitive healers have embraced the idea that animals have souls. Anyone who has truly loved a pet knows they are not just animals—they are sentient beings filled with emotions, intelligence, and an ability to love deeply.

As an animal communicator, I've personally connected with pets and feel deeply blessed by those experiences. They share with me their continued presence, offering messages of comfort, joy, and even humour to their grieving guardians. These encounters reaffirm that our pets do not simply vanish after death. Instead, they transition into a different state of being, one where they are still very much a part of our lives.

Many pet parents worry about whether their pet has found peace or if they are still suffering in some way. I assure you that when a pet passes, their soul is freed from any pain or suffering they may have experienced in their final moments. They do not carry regret, anger, or sorrow. Instead, they are surrounded by pure love and light. Their spirit remains intact, watching over you with the same devotion they had in life.

Do Pets Reincarnate? What You Need to Know

One of the most common questions I am asked is: "Can my pet come back to me?"

The concept of reincarnation suggests that souls return to experience life again, sometimes in different forms, sometimes in familiar ones. Just as human souls may choose to return for further learning and growth, animals, too, may reincarnate for reasons of love, purpose, or connection.

In my sessions, I have encountered countless stories of pets who return to their guardians in different bodies—sometimes as another dog or cat or a different species altogether. There are common signs that may indicate a reincarnated pet:

Uncanny Similarities: A new pet displaying mannerisms, habits, or personality traits identical to a past pet.

Instant Connection: A deep, immediate bond that feels like you have known them forever.

Reactions to Familiar Places: A pet recognising a home, routine, or even responding to their old name.

You bring a new puppy home, and they walk straight in the door and head over to their old bed!

When a soul chooses to return, it does so out of love. Some pets return quickly, as if they cannot bear to be apart from their guardian for long. Others wait years before re-entering the physical world. Some may not return but instead act as a guide from the spirit realm.

It's essential to trust your intuition. If you deeply know that a new pet carries the essence of a past companion, honour that feeling. Whether they return physically or remain as a loving presence in spirit, they are never truly gone.

How Souls Continue Their Journey After Death

Death is not an end—it is a transition. The physical body is temporary, but the soul is eternal.

In my work, I have been privileged to witness the continued journey of pets beyond this life. They often describe a place of peace and beauty, a realm of light where they are free to run, play, and rest. Other animals meet them, loved ones who have passed, and even spirit guides who assist them in their transition. There is no loneliness, no fear—only love.

Some pets take on roles as spirit guides, offering comfort and wisdom to their guardians from beyond. They may appear in dreams, leave signs, or send feelings of warmth and reassurance. Have you ever felt your pet's presence, even after they have passed? A sudden whiff of their familiar scent, a fleeting shadow in the corner of your eye. These are not coincidences. These are the gentle reminders that they are still with you, loving you as fiercely as they did in life.

Another way they continue their journey is by helping guide new pets into your life. They may orchestrate events that bring you to an animal in need, nudging your heart to open again. This is not a replacement but a continuation of love in a new form.

Connecting with Your Pet Beyond the Physical World

Your bond with your pet was built on love, and love does not die. Even though their body is gone, your connection remains strong. There are ways you can continue to feel their presence and communicate with them:

1. Pay Attention to Signs - Pets in spirit love to send signs. These might come as:

> Seeing their name in unexpected places.

> Finding feathers, coins, or objects they were fond of.

Sensing their energy, hearing their paws on the floor, or feeling their warmth beside you are just some of the ways our pets in spirit make their presence known. One message that made me smile came from a dog who weighed over 40kg. He told me to reassure his guardian that he would show her he was still around when she least expected it. I asked her if he used to lean into her, and she said yes, though we both didn't think much of it then.

About a month later, she returned to tell me that while standing in the paddock watching her horses, she suddenly felt a heavy weight press against her legs, so strongly that her knees nearly buckled. At that moment, she knew without a doubt that it was him.

Be open to receiving these signs and acknowledge them when they come. Let your pet know you see and feel them.

2. Visit Them in Dreams - Dreams are a powerful place for spiritual connection. Many pet parents report vivid dreams where their beloved animal visits them, offering comfort and reassurance. Before you sleep, set the intention to come to you in dreamtime. Keep a journal by your bed and write down any dreams you remember.

3. Talk to Them - They are always listening to you. Just because you can't see them doesn't mean they can't hear you. Speak to your pet as you always did. Share your day, tell them you love them, and ask them for guidance. Their energy is still present, and they will respond in ways that you will feel in your heart.

4. Trust Your Intuition - Your heart knows when they are near. The feeling of comfort, the sudden warmth, the knowing that they are with you is real. Trust in your connection and know that love transcends all barriers.

Love Never Ends

Losing a pet is one of the most challenging experiences we face, but their journey does not end with death. They are still here, loving, guiding, and watching over you. Whether they reincarnate, send signs, visit in dreams, or remain as a warm presence in your heart, they are never truly gone.

Your pet's love for you is eternal. As you move forward, know that they are still walking beside you, just as they always have, in a different way. The bond you shared is unbreakable, and the soul's journey continues— always, and forever.

Old Friends, New Beginnings

Losing Harvey so suddenly broke us in ways I can't fully describe. Harvey wasn't just any dog—he was my husband's heart dog. And at only 7.5 years of age, our gorgeous boy was still so full of life. He seemed healthy and happy, his usual cheeky self. We had no idea anything was wrong.

Until one early morning in late October 2024, I woke to the sound of him struggling to breathe. We rushed him to the vet. He was sedated straight away. And then the words came—jarring and heavy: A mass on his soft palate. His airway nearly closed. His throat and lungs were filled with pus. There were talks of a seven-day induced coma. A possible tracheotomy. And in that heartbreaking moment, my husband and I knew. We made the decision no one ever wants to face—but we made it with love and as gently as we could.

It all happened so fast. One minute, he was part of our everyday. The next, we searched for answers in the stillness he left behind. And while the veterinary team was kind and compassionate, I knew deep in my gut that they couldn't give me the closure my heart was aching for. I needed something different. Something deeper. Something that made space for the soul connection we had with him.

That's when I found Donna.

From the moment our session started, I felt something was different. But there was one moment that truly cracked me wide open. Donna paused and asked, "Sarah, do you ever say the phrase 'I don't have time to f*ck around'?"

My husband, who, to be clear, is the most sceptical human on the planet, immediately burst out laughing. And I said, "Donna ... if you knew me, you'd know I say that almost daily."

Harvey had been listening. And that was his way of letting me know that he had heard me and was still around—and already planning his return. His little body had failed him without warning, and true to form, he didn't have time to f*ck around either.

The comfort that session gave me was like exhaling for the first time in days. It softened something inside me that had gone hard with shock and grief.

So, when my own heart dog, Kali, passed away just two and a half months later—this time from end-stage renal failure—there was no question. Donna was the first person I called.

And again, in that space between worlds, she brought through the most grounding, goosebump-inducing message. She said, "Kali doesn't think you can do this without her." Those were the words I'd whispered to Kali just before she passed.

She also told me that, like Harvey, Kali was coming back. And soon. That our work together wasn't done. That she couldn't do it in the body she had—but she wasn't going far. Or for long. And just like that, my heart cracked open again, not just with grief, but with something softer. Hope.

After going from a three-dog household to just one in under three months, the silence hit us hard. Doug, our remaining dog, was lost without his companions—and if I'm honest, so were we. The house felt too still. Too quiet. There was a space where joy used to live, and we felt it in every corner.

So, we decided to welcome a new little soul into our family. At the end of February, we flew to Sydney to meet a litter of Pug puppies. I held each one gently in my arms, taking a moment to connect with them—to really feel into it. With each tiny body I cradled, I quietly asked, "Are you the one?"

And then it happened. I picked up one particular little boy and heard it—soft, subtle, and completely clear: "This one." I couldn't tell you where the voice came from. But here's the wild part: my husband heard it too. That was it. We knew.

And so, in mid-March, the little whirlwind now known as Floyd joined our family.

Cheeky, wild, impossibly cute, and full of character … Floyd blew in like a mini Pug cyclone.

And I found myself wondering: "Is this Kali coming back? Could it really be her? And how would I know?"

Floyd travelled up from the breeder via a special pet transport company, and after two full days on the road, he was finally arriving. We were so excited that we arrived early at the café next to the meeting point. We ordered coffee, sat, waited, and grinned like kids on Christmas Eve.

And then the message came: "They've arrived." I reached for my purse. And in that exact moment, something flew out—literally popped out of a zipped inner pocket I hadn't opened.

It was the pendant that holds Kali's ashes. The one I'd carried with me every day since she passed. Tucked away. Hidden. And yet, there it was—out in the open, as if to say: "I'm here."

I froze, and my breath caught.

Stunned, we made our way to the meeting point. Floyd was handed over to us, all wide eyes and soft fur, and we gently walked him to the car. We'd come prepared with a special waterproof blanket—affectionately known in our house as "the Kali blanket." It had travelled everywhere with her in those last few months. It had soaked up a lot more than just accidents; it had soaked up moments, memories, grief. And now, here it was again, waiting for a new little body.

I climbed into the car, draped the Kali blanket across my lap, and my husband carefully passed Floyd through to me. The moment he landed in my lap, he paused. He sniffed the blanket slowly, almost thoughtfully. Then suddenly, he stopped, turned, looked straight up at me and launched into my arms, tail wagging so wildly it could've powered the car. He covered my face in kisses like he'd known me forever.

And in that exact moment, my heart whispered: "It's her."

It wasn't the cautious curiosity of a new puppy. It was the joyful, emotional homecoming of an old friend.

From that moment on, I've felt Kali's spirit right there, woven into Floyd. And while Floyd is very much his own person—with his own quirks, chaos, and personality—there are moments where Kali shines through so clearly, it takes my breath away.

He's picked up cues and training like he's done it all before. He joined me for a professional photo shoot two days after arriving home. A week later, he was on national television—cool, calm, collected, like he'd been doing it for years. And as Kali, he had.

Kali had been by my side in media interviews, featured in magazines, and even appeared on Better Homes and Gardens. She was always more than just a dog—she was my partner and co-pilot in everything I did. And now, somehow, it feels like she's back.

Not just in spirit, but in energy, in essence.

There's a sense of peace that sits with me now. A calm certainty that I'm not alone.

That she never really left. Even when she's not physically here, she is.

It's a strange and beautiful thing, this journey of grief and connection. Losing Harvey and Kali broke something open in me. But finding Floyd—and the feeling of Kali coming back through him—has healed something, too.

Donna helped me bridge that impossible gap between heartbreak and hope. She gave me a way to hear what my heart already knew. And for that, I'll be forever grateful.

Chapter 18

Can I Really Communicate With My Pet In Spirit?

The heartbreak of saying goodbye to a cherished companion often leaves us with one aching question: "Is my pet still with me?" The answer, in my experience, is a heartfelt yes. Our beloved animals remain close, offering comfort, sending signs, and continuing their connection with us beyond the physical. The true challenge isn't whether they're reaching out — it's whether our hearts are open enough to recognise the subtle ways they show up.

Understanding Animal Communication

I believe everyone has the ability to communicate with their pets in spirit. People connect with their pets all the time without realising it. Have you ever found yourself suddenly thinking about your pet or instinctively doing something that reminds you of them? Perhaps you've walked to the cupboard, opened the door, and started handing out treats without knowing why, only to realise later that your pet used to ask for them at that very time. These subtle moments of intuition are how your pet continues to connect with you.

Animal communication is a natural ability that we all possess. Some people may be more naturally attuned to it, while others develop their sensitivity through practice and trust. The key is to quiet the logical mind and allow the heart and intuition to lead.

How to Tune into Your Intuition

We all have intuitive abilities, even if we don't always recognise them. When communicating with animals— either living or those in spirit—we use our intuitive senses, often referred to as the "Clairs":

- **Clairvoyance (seeing):** Receiving images, symbols, or visual impressions.

- **Clairaudience (hearing):** Hearing words, phrases, or sounds in your mind.

- **Clairsentience (feeling):** Sensing emotions or physical sensations.

- **Clairtangency (touching):** Feeling an energetic presence or sensation.

- **Claircognizance (knowing):** Having an unexplainable inner knowing.

Two additional senses that play an essential role in communicating with pets:

- **Clairalience (smell):** The ability to "smell" things that are not physically present.

- **Clairgustance (taste):** The ability to "taste" something without physically consuming it.

Some naturally experience one or two of these abilities, while others use a combination. With practice—or better yet, play—you can strengthen these connections and recognise how your pet may reach out to you.

When I first started communicating with animals, I didn't realise I was using all of my senses. I remember one day describing what I was seeing, smelling, and tasting, and it suddenly hit me—I was far more connected than I had ever known. That moment changed everything for me.

The best way to "turn on" your intuitive senses is through play. Notice I didn't say *practice*—because that sounds like work! Tuning into your senses should be fun, and there are so many playful ways to awaken them. The more you relax and enjoy the process, the easier it becomes to recognise the subtle ways animals—especially those in spirit—communicate with you.

Playing with Your Intuitive Senses

A simple way to play with your "clairs" is to walk through a garden, by the water's edge, or in an open paddock. Close your eyes and ask yourself:

- **What do I "see"?** Mentally take note of what images come to mind. You may recall the flowers, trees, or even an animal nearby.

- **What do I "hear"?** At first, you might notice traffic or background noise, but as you relax, you'll start to hear subtler sounds—the hum of bees, birds chirping, a dog barking in the distance.

- **What do I "smell"?** Let scents drift to you. If you're near flowers, you might catch their fragrance. Consider how often pets stop to "sniff the air"—allow yourself to do the same.

- **What do I "taste"?** This one can be surprising! I once worked with a dog outside in a paddock, sharing what he saw, heard, and smelled. Then—he licked cow poo! And just like that, I got the taste in my mouth. I'll never forget it!

Keep playing. Ask yourself: **What do I feel? What do I know?** I often do this during my morning walks—it awakens all my senses for the day ahead.

If you don't have time for a walk, try this fun exercise: Imagine cutting a lemon. Picture it vividly—its bright colour, the way the juice squirts as you slice it. Can you taste the sourness? Smell the citrus? My face tingles as I write this, and I can almost taste the bitterness! Once you master the lemon, try chocolate or a freshly baked cookie.

Tuning into your intuition doesn't have to be hard—make it a game, make it fun! And if that little skeptic in your mind tells you that you can't do this, push it aside and know that you can!

"Want to learn how to connect with your Pets in Spirit. Be sure to check out my website or visit my Facebook page to see what's coming up next!"

Practical Exercises to Connect with Your Pet

1. Automatic Writing Exercise

A simple way to tune into your pet's messages is through automatic writing. This exercise helps quiet the mind and allows messages to flow naturally.

- Find a quiet space outdoors where you can ground yourself.
- Walk barefoot on the grass, feeling the connection to the earth.
- Sit in a comfortable position with a pen and journal.
- Close your eyes, take deep breaths, and centre yourself.
- Open your journal and begin writing, without overthinking.
- Once you feel comfortable, ask your pet a simple question: "Good morning, [pet's name], do you have a message for me today?"
- Let your pen flow freely—don't judge, edit, or question your writing.

With practice, you'll notice patterns, phrases, or even specific words that resonate deeply. These are messages from your pet.

2. Dream Visitations

One of the most profound ways pets communicate is through dreams. Before going to bed, try this simple technique:

- Sit on the edge of your bed with your feet on the floor.
- Close your eyes and visualise your pet in your mind's eye.
- Silently or aloud, invite them to visit you in your dreams: "[Pet's name], please come to me tonight with a message."
- Go to sleep with an open heart.
- When you wake, write down anything you receive.

Many people report vivid dreams of feeling, hearing, or seeing their pet. Sometimes, the pet may not appear directly but may send symbolic messages, such as running through a field, wagging their tail, or simply sitting beside you.

3. Using Oracle Cards to Receive Messages

Oracle cards can be a wonderful tool for receiving messages from your pet. You don't need to be an expert; follow your intuition.

- Choose an oracle or animal spirit deck that resonates with you.
- Sit quietly with the deck, take a deep breath, and focus on your pet.
- Ask a question, such as: "What message does my pet have for me today?"
- Shuffle the deck and draw a card.
- Pay attention to the imagery, words, and any feelings that arise.

Your pet may use the card to convey love, reassurance, or guidance.

Be sure to check out my Oracle Cards and Journals at

www.petlossandgrief.com/shop

What Is Animal Communication and How Can It Help?

Animal communication is a beautiful and deeply healing bridge between this world and the next, allowing pet parents to reconnect with their beloved companions in spirit. As an Animal Communicator—sometimes called a Pet Psychic or Pet Medium—I intuitively connect with pets who have crossed over, receiving their thoughts, emotions, and messages of love. These sessions offer reassurance that your pet's soul continues its journey, connected to you by a profound and unbreakable bond. Whether through images, feelings, sensations, or words, your pet's essence shines through bringing comfort, guidance, and often a spark of their familiar personality.

An animal communicator facilitating a session can bring deep emotional healing and peace. Grief can feel overwhelming, especially when there are lingering questions, guilt, or simply a longing to know your pet is okay. Messages from your pet may bring clarity, offer reassurance, or remind you that they are still by your side in spirit. These moments of connection validate that your love hasn't ended—it's changed form.

I've had the privilege of connecting with hundreds of pets in spirit, each with their unique personality, love, and wisdom to share. While some may question the idea of life after death or the possibility of connecting with a pet beyond the physical world, those who have experienced this work firsthand know the comfort and peace it can bring. A session with an animal communicator isn't about proving anything—it's about love, healing, and celebrating the enduring bond between you and your pet.

If you choose to reach out to your beloved companion in spirit, bring your sense of adventure, an open heart, and maybe a box of tissues. These sessions often spark laughter, tears, and powerful moments of recognition that remind you your pet is still near. Energy flows best when you welcome it—if you carry fear or heavy scepticism, you may struggle to connect clearly with your pet. Trust in the love that never fades, and you may receive a message that stays with you for the rest of your life.

Here are some of the ways animal communication may support you:

- **Closure and Understanding**: Messages from your pet can offer comfort and a sense of peace, especially if you weren't able to say goodbye.

- **Improved Relationships**: Sessions can help you better understand and support your surviving pets through their grief.

- **Emotional Support**: The process can be cathartic, offering a safe space to share your feelings and receive empathy.

- **Messages from the Pet**: Many people find healing in receiving heartfelt messages—expressions of love, forgiveness, or reassurance that their pet is at peace.

While not everyone will believe in animal communication, many who do find it to be a gentle, transformative experience. At its heart, it's about love, connection, and honouring the life and spirit of your cherished companion.

https://bookme.name/donnadolittle/ - to book a session

Or visit my website to learn more at:

www.donnadolittle.com.au

Wentworth & Griffin

Losing any family member is difficult at the best of times, but for me, having to send my two precious boys, Wentworth and Griffin (pugs), over the rainbow bridge has been the hardest thing I have ever had to do. Griffin grew his angel wings on 26 October 2022, aged 7 years, 6 months, and 6 days. Wentworth grew his angel wings on 21 July 2023, aged 8 years, 10 months, and 19 days. I have been Wentworth and Griffin's mumma since they were 8 weeks old. These dates and their birthdays are days when I focus on my memories of them, more than ever.

I carried so much guilt when I had to make the heartbreaking decision to let them cross the rainbow bridge. I had so many unanswered questions - Why couldn't I save my boys? Why was I such a bad mumma? Do they forgive me? Are they happy over the rainbow bridge? What messages do they have for me?

I still cry for my boys, but Donna's communications bring me so much comfort. Through her gift, she has been able to connect me to both my boys, they send me messages through Donna that have helped me so much through my loss and my grief. Hearing from Donna, their little quirks that only I know of, makes me know that they want me to heal and work through my guilt.

Without Donna's support, through her communications, I know I would still be bargaining with myself and not have become a foster mumma for pugs on their transition to their furever home. But importantly, Poppy and Eddy would not have chosen me to be their mumma in their senior years.

> I believe Wentworth and Griffin have made these things happen for me, to bring joy and love back into my life. I can't forget to mention Penny and Ruby, too.

Signs Your Pet is Sending You Messages

Even if you don't experience direct communication, your pet always finds ways to reach you. Here are some common signs:

- **Feeling their presence:** A sudden warm sensation or the feeling of them brushing against you.

- **Hearing their sounds:** The familiar sound of their collar jingling, paws padding on the floor, or a soft sigh.

- **Seeing their image:** A fleeting shadow, a vision in meditation, or an unexpected photograph appearing.

- **Finding their favourite things:** Their toys, blankets, or objects moving unexpectedly.

- **Noticing repeating symbols:** Butterflies, feathers, rainbows, or numbers that remind you of them.

- **Sensing their energy in a special place:** Feeling their presence in their favourite spot in the house.

Overcoming Doubt and Trusting the Connection

It's natural to be sceptical. Many people dismiss their experiences, thinking, "I'm just imagining this." But the truth is, real messages from pets often carry an undeniable sense of knowing, warmth, and comfort.

I have received so much evidence from pets in spirit that I no longer question the reality of these connections. Messages that contain specific details—things only the pet's guardian could know—have repeatedly reinforced that our pets continue to be with us.

If you're struggling with doubt, remember this: Your pet wants to connect with you. They are patient, loving, and persistent. Trust that what you feel, see, and hear is real.

Finding Comfort in Spiritual Connections

Your bond with your pet didn't end when they passed. Their soul is still intertwined with yours, and they continue to support and love you from beyond. Please take comfort in knowing that they are never truly gone.

The more you practice tuning into your intuition, the more natural it will feel to communicate with your pet. Keep an open heart, trust what you receive, and find peace knowing that love transcends the physical world.

Your pet is still with you. They always will be.

"I didn't leave you — I just changed form. I'm still by your side, just softer now."

A Journey Of Love And Healing

*"Your love was a light in my darkest hours,
a warmth that shielded me from fear.
And with you by my side, I learned to be fearless.
You loved me fiercely, without hesitation,
which gave me bravery I never knew I had".
~ Nadia*

The Everlasting Bond with Your Pet

As we come to the final pages of this book, it's important to remember this is not an end, but a gentle pause in the ongoing journey you share with your beloved pet.

The bond you have built together—through the joy, laughter, quiet companionship, and even through the grief—is not something that disappears. It transforms. It deepens. It continues.

That love remains whether your pet is still physically with you or has transitioned into spirit. It is present in your memories, the little signs and whispers, and the moments when you feel their energy brush against your heart. Love like this is not bound by time, space, or even lifetimes.

Finding Strength in the Grieving Process

Grief is not a problem to fix—it's a natural, sacred response to love. It comes in waves, sometimes crashing, sometimes still and silent. But every tear you've cried, every ache you've felt, reflects how deeply you've loved.

You've now walked through some of this journey's darkest, most tender parts. You've faced questions with no easy answers, sat in the discomfort of loss, and perhaps even discovered that healing isn't about "getting over" your pet, but learning to carry them with you in a new way.

Along the way, you've also met stories of connection, soul bonds stretching beyond the veil, and pets returning in new bodies to continue their journey with the humans they love. You've learned to listen with your heart. To trust the subtle. To honour the invisible threads that bind you still.

And through it all, you've shown incredible strength—even when you didn't feel strong.

Resources for Continued Support

Please know that you are not alone.

Support exists in many forms:

- Trusted animal communicators who can help bridge the gap between worlds.

- Grief counsellors and pet loss support groups offer safe spaces to express your sorrow.

- Rituals, memorials, and quiet moments honouring your pet's life and presence.

- Books, communities, and spiritual guidance to help you explore what lies beyond.

If you're still navigating the storm, lean on these supports. Reach out. Speak their name. Let others witness your love and your grief.

You do not need to walk this path alone.

A Final Message Of Comfort And Hope

Dear reader, if you take one thing with you from these pages, let it be this:

Your journey with your pet is not over.

It may look different now. It may be softer, quieter, more inward. But it is *still happening*. Every memory, every dream, every sign is part of that continuing connection.

Grief and love exist side by side. And over time, the grief softens, while the love grows even stronger. Many have found that their pets find ways to return—sometimes in a new form, sometimes simply as a presence that never truly leaves. That is not wishful thinking; it is the language of the soul.

As you move forward, carry this truth in your heart:

Your pet loved you then. They love you now. And they will love you always.

This is a journey of love.
A journey of healing.
A journey that never truly ends.

Thank you for allowing me to walk this part of the path with you.

With deepest love and understanding,
Donna

Final Message From Ajax

It's with tears in my eyes that I share this message from my beautiful soul dog, Ajax. He came to me as I slept—his presence as strong and loving as ever—and he whispered, *"It's time to share my message to help support you on this journey."*

I couldn't ignore the nudge to write this book. Ajax, my beloved companion and guiding light, knew that to heal my own heart, I needed to share what I've learned from walking beside hundreds of grieving pet parents. Parents whose hearts were shattered. Who wondered if they would ever feel whole again.

I've spent countless hours writing… rewriting… adding a little here, taking a little there. Just when I thought it was done, Ajax arrived in the quiet of the night to remind me: *"There's more. This part is for you—and for them."*

And so it began to flow…

> *I knew I was sick long before you realised. Before you even go there, no, you weren't a bad pet parent. You did everything right. The moment you sensed something was wrong, your heart kicked into protection mode, desperate to fix it. There was nothing to fix. My body was tired, and my soul knew it was time to go. I didn't want you to carry the burden of knowing too soon. I kept it to myself for as long*

as I could. I knew I could help you better from the other side, and I wouldn't be a burden by this failing body.

When you're sad ... when you wonder if I'm near ... I sprinkle a little magic. A feather. A rainbow. A moment that makes you laugh. And you always talk to me. I love when you talk to me. Don't ever stop. I'm always with you.

After I passed, my first mission was to send you another dog—one to keep you busy.

(Yes, I can hear you laughing at that.)

You needed someone a little bit cheeky ... someone to challenge you, to keep you out of the depths of grief. I watched as you stopped eating, stopped moving, and questioned everything—even your gift of animal communication. You asked, "How could I not have known?" But mum, you did. You just weren't meant to carry that knowing then. It would have changed the journey.

Snowy was always meant for you. Giving you another Golden, though I know how deeply you love them, wouldn't have helped you grow. Snowy came into your life with purpose, just like I did. He's here to love you, in a different way. To support your soul's path. And don't worry—I'm guiding him.

He snuggles with you at night and helps you feel safe again. He's my little messenger, sent straight from me to you.

I know it all happened fast. You were torn apart, trying to find a way to save me. But I was quietly sending you messages—"Let me go with dignity, I don't wish to keep fighting." On that Friday, we took our last walk. We lay together on the grass. I even ate a little dinner. You felt hope, but I was already saying goodbye. That was the last time I licked your face, the last time I looked into your eyes in this lifetime.

For those 48 hours, you didn't leave my side. You made a little bed and we all cuddle together. I felt every ounce of your love. And I chuckled when Lil Jess tried to sneak a taste of whatever you were giving me to keep me going. She knew, too. She stayed a little longer just for you—until Snowy was ready to take up the mantle.

Your love kept me going. Your energy gave me strength. It flowed from your heart to mine, lifting me as I crossed into the spirit world.

My dearest one… our bond is eternal. It didn't end when I left my body—it only deepened.

I am with you. Always.

And I honour your courage for sharing this message—for letting our love story help others on their journey.

**Forever yours,
Your special boy, Ajax**

"Some angels choose fur instead of wings, and when they leave, they don't take our love with them—they leave it behind to guide us."

My Gifts To You

Access Your Support Bonuses using the link below or QR code

https://petlossandgrief.com/book-goodies/

www.ingramcontent.com/pod-product-compliance
Lightning Source LLC
Chambersburg PA
CBHW072021070526
44583CB00015B/1576